The Other Side of the Table

Books by Mary J. Shafer
Be Fruitful and Multiply
Two Shall Be One
When in Doubt

The Other Side of the Table

Mary J. Shafer

ISBN: 978-1451585391

Cover design: Stephanie C. Shafer

Printed in the United States of America

Author may be contacted at mjshafer@cox.net

Contents

Acknowledgements

When you begin to write a story that is close to your heart, you inevitably think of the many individuals who touched you in the process. I am so grateful to friends who stood by me in the midst of upheaval. Also, to the countless others on the fringes who provided a hug – saying with that simple gesture what I knew they dare not speak. When you are destined to walk the road less traveled, it is a blessing to see the warm smile of a friend beside you.

I thank my parents for always stressing hard work and dedication to a goal. They have always inspired me. I am grateful to my siblings, my husband and my four wonderful children. Without my children I never would have learned what "the other side of the table" felt like. It is a lesson, so valuable and has helped me grow professionally and personally. My children continue to demonstrate that every child is "gifted" in their own unique way. It is up to us as parents and educators to find each child's unique gifts and do our best to nurture them.

I sincerely thank every educator who ever crossed paths with my children, for doing what they thought was best. Teachers often have few resources and lack the support they need to be effective for students and families. Most do the best with what they have.

Above all, I thank God who always leads me where I need to go and gives me strength for the journey. He puts the words on the page with clarity and purpose. Without Him this book never would have been written. Where He leads, I will follow.

And finally, I thank you, the reader. Thanks for taking a chance on an unknown author. Many have encouraged me to "keep writing" so, God willing, there will be more books. Maybe someday my name will be bigger than the title. That is the mark of success in writing. I pray that I will always have gratitude and humility. These are truly the markings of success in life. Live your life with purpose and never let any person or situation steal your joy. In the words of Mother Teresa: "In the end it is between you and God. It was never really between you and them anyway."

Introduction

This all started because I felt a nagging desire to write my fourth book. I have written books before – three to be exact. The first one was humorous, the second inspirational and the third another attempt at humor. When I knew it was time to write my fourth, I thought it should be inspirational, humorous or maybe a mixture of both. It is what I am good at. At least people have told me that – and I believe them because not all of them are close friends. Some are actually strangers who just needed a laugh or something to believe in at the same time that I did.

Feeling this pull towards the computer, I sat down over the course of a week and started several versions of what would be mediocre books but not the book that I felt compelled to write. *The Other Side of the Table* kept popping into my head, threatening to jump onto the computer screen. Not strained and difficult like the other stories I was desperately trying to extract. This idea was not a new concept. I had thought about writing it many times in the last few years but was too caught up in the emotional aftermath to even begin to think it was a good idea. After all, I had lived it. Shouldn't that be enough for any rational person? So, finally, I stopped pushing the words away, accepted the fact that sometimes I'm anything but rational and let it flow. It was time to tell it, as only I could.

I believe other parents may benefit from this story that needs to be told. I'm not sure why I am always so determined to help others but I know enough about psychology to know there is probably some underlying Freudian reason. I know when something needs to be done, I feel compelled to do it. Sometimes I really wish someone else would do it. But after prayerful consideration, I realize the job is mine alone. So, I have come to the conclusion that this book was meant to be written. I wrote it for myself as well as for every professional who has flip-flopped between emotional comfort and sound, professional knowledge. I wrote it for every mother who might face a similar challenge. It is written from my perspective and every situation is based on facts as they occurred. The names of people and places have been altered to protect the privacy of the individuals. I sincerely tried to be fair to everyone who played a part. Inevitably, I have sat in their seats at some point. My sincere intention is to educate about a different perspective, not to find fault with people who I know did their best with what they knew at the time. After all, these people were like family.

I believe we all learn from whatever seat we are currently occupying. I know I've learned more than I can ever put into words. Some days I am amazed to still stumble over a new lesson, three years later. Intellectually, I know life is a learning process. Emotionally, there are times when something mundane reminds me of the saga and buried feelings threaten to surface. It's then that I dig deep and remind myself that I am a better mother and a more competent professional because of the road I was meant to walk. A road where lessons were learned, friends lived the definition of that word, and faith grew by leaps and bounds. That is a gift, any way you look at it and I am blessed beyond words.

I am a school psychologist by profession and have been one for a little over twenty years. I received a Masters of Education and an Educational Specialist degree from Kent State University in 1986 and 1987, respectively. Being a school psychologist is as much a part of me today as my hair color or my height. It is more than a career – it is my life. It defines who I am and the basic truths I've come to believe in. This role has brought me infinite joy but also unsolicited frustration. There have been times in my life when I wished I was anything but a school psychologist. Days I would rather have turned a blind eye to trouble I saw brewing on the educational horizon. Times I wish it wasn't so imbedded in the essence of who I am. I know there are days when my four children wish they had "just a regular mom." A mom, who knew less about education or, at the very least, was less outspoken about it. There have been times when they would share some story about school and then cringe, wondering if I would call their teachers about some questionable practice. Until recently they attended a private, religious school and I worked in a similar school. I knew how things worked there, or how they should work anyway. That was sometimes too close for comfort. They have warned me with, "I'm only telling you this if you promise not to call." I think over the years we have reached a mutual understanding about school. They feel comfortable telling me most things and I pick my battles wisely. Not every tiny incident is worth going to war over, but I detest apathy. I believe if you are not part of the solution, you're part of the problem. My children know I will always take a firm stand for children and families if someone needs to. Too few people do. People talk, but sadly, they seldom walk. That is not me.

Yes, there are times when ignorance can be a wonderful cocoon. It insulates us and keeps us in our safe, predictable world. I'll be the first to admit, there are days when I've longed for ignorance. I've longed to be content with mediocrity. I've questioned why I can't just settle like so many others I see, choosing to put on blinders and bite their tongues. Not settling has cost me sleep, security, income and friendships. It has pulled me out of my comfort zone while also propelling me to new heights. On challenging days, I've taken solace in the lyrics of a popular song, "It's not easy to be me." However, when I look in the mirror at the end of each day I am proud of the road I continue to walk. It is the road less traveled but I firmly believe it was the road chosen for me, and so I follow, wherever destiny leads.

Chapter 1

In the Beginning

"What the heck is the kid doing?" I thought as the first grade boy got up and turned his chair completely around. He now sat with his back to me and proceeded to repeat the numbers I had just recited from my booklet.

"Five, three, six, one, nine."

Baffled, I asked, "What are you doing, Jack?"

"You said to say the numbers backwards, didn't you?"

Of course I did, silly me! Thus began another fun-filled day in the life of a school psychologist.

I went into school psychology because it seemed like an interesting profession. The catalog said something like "a school psychologist works with children who are experiencing difficulty in the regular classroom setting." That sounds intriguing, I thought. A little more than a classroom teacher but the same school schedule I had grown to know and love. I've always loved children and knew any career I chose must revolve around them. I also love psychology and delving into the workings of the mind. I've always known I was destined to help people in some way. I was born the helpful type. I am third in a family of four which inevitably explains it all. I was also raised in a religious home and am raising my children that way which may partly explain my charitable attitude. Some years ago I read that my birth order dictated being helpful. I thoroughly embraced the role at a young age. As a young girl in the 70's I actually liked unloading the dishwasher, folding clothes, helping my younger brother with homework. This has served me well over the years and fostered organization. My mother, now in her seventies, still talks about how helpful I've always been. In the end I found school psychology, or maybe it found me. It is, after all, a "helping profession." Yes, I'm sure it was a match made in heaven, literally.

After receiving my Educational Specialist degree in school psychology from Kent State, I accepted a position with a private company that supplied school psychologists, speech and language pathologists and nurses to private schools in the Cleveland area. Because of the nature of school psychology, typically you are assigned to a particular school for anywhere from one to three days a week. A five day a week school is very rare. So, since I wanted to work full time, I was assigned two or three schools those first few years. In the beginning it was hard to keep track of where I was expected on a particular day, but I soon fell into a routine. I pride myself on being a quick study.

These first few years, I was single. I did not make much money but I loved it anyway. Money has never been a big incentive for me. As long as I have enough of it to get by, I am fine. In retrospect, I didn't have many bills either. I lived in a small efficiency apartment and drove a used car. Dinner was mostly macaroni and cheese or dinner with a blind date I went on to please Mom and at least look like I was trying to find a husband. School psychology was fresh and new to me back then. It was exciting with a zero risk factor. After all these were someone else' kids I was working with. Whatever advice I doled out would not affect my livelihood in the least. I didn't stress over many of the decisions I was asked to consult with teachers about, or often make on my own. I knew that I did the best with the information I had at the time and the recommended accommodations or placement decisions would work out fine for these students. After all, that's what the textbooks said and my emotional investment was minimal if anything. Yes, I slept fairly well my first few years as a school psychologist.

My biggest worry in my early days as a school psychologist was whether or not I would be taken seriously. Most of the teachers I was working with were older than me and many had families. I also had no teaching experience which caused some of them to question my credibility. Although you don't have to have a teaching degree to be a school psychologist, many people do. Many seem to enter school psychology after having taught for years and either admiring school psychologists or thinking they could do a better job. Either way, many teachers were skeptical of a "newbie" school psychologist who was the age of some of their own children. Some of the older teachers actually made derogatory comments behind my back like "what could she possibly know." Apparently the advanced degree in education meant nothing if I hadn't given birth – yet. Yes, those first few years in my profession it was a tough road, but I was ready. I've always been well equipped with a "bring it on" type of attitude. My dad instilled in each of his four children the mind set of "when the going gets tough... the tough get going." Yes, anything was possible with the right attitude and hard work. My dad, who passed away twenty five years ago, was one of my first, and always my best teacher.

So, although I met with some skepticism in those early years, I approached my job with a sincere desire to be the best I could be and learn all I could learn. I've never been one to think I know it all. I knew these seasoned teachers had as much knowledge to share with me as I could share with them. Knowledge is not all about what you read in books. Hands-on experience is one of the best teachers and I was smart enough to know that I did not have that at this point in my career. I believe every situation in life is a learning experience if you are open to growth. I believe anyone who thinks they know it all is a fooling themselves and trying desperately to fool everyone around them. With this attitude in mind, I made friends in my new school setting rather quickly. If nothing else, people readily warmed up to me, and gaining people's trust is half the battle in school psychology. Maybe this is when I first learned "people don't care what you know unless they know that you care." Many so called "professionals" would be well served if they humbled themselves and remembered this crucial bit of wisdom.

I also learned another important fact in those early years. School psychology is what an individual and a setting choose to make it. Strictly defined, it encompasses "conducting educational evaluations for academic placement and consulting with teachers and parents about the educational needs of students". It can involve group and individual counseling also but these are luxuries many school psychologists do not have time for. It is largely a public relations job. If you have good people skills and want to expand on your role, you can "sell yourself" to teachers, administrators and parents and delve into non-traditional roles. In the early years I was comfortable with just testing and was not very comfortable with the public relations part of the job. Some people never become good at this and thus their role is limited, either by choice, by the limits of their personalities or by reins of the administration. Over the years I have embraced the public relations aspect of school psychology, proven myself to several principals and thus been assigned non-traditional duties. I am confident that at the peak of my career, I am a very valued employee at the schools that called me their school psychologist. I am known by parents, teachers and administrators as someone they can count on to stand up for students and know what was in their best interests. Yes, I believe that most of the time, people respect my opinion. That is always a wonderful compliment, and one I never take lightly.

School psychology can be a lonely profession. It is different from teaching in that way. Teachers have other people they can bounce ideas off of if they need to. A school psychologist is the only one in a school who knows the job. School psychologists can bounce ideas off of other school psychologists but no one knows their building, their principal and the teachers they are working with, so resources are minimal. This can be a good and a bad thing. I have seen some people thrive under these circumstances and some people do next to nothing. Self-motivation is the key. You have to love what you are doing and do your best with it. By the nature of the job, you are often stuck in a small office by yourself. This office is usually tucked away in some corner. When I did my internship, which is required before becoming a real school psychologist, I worked in a bathroom that was no longer used in a large public school system. That provided some comic relief and some embarrassment for students as well as me. The first time I was asked to reevaluate a twelve year old boy and walked him into the door that clearly said, "girls" he looked up in horror and proclaimed, "I'm not going in there, no way!" When I explained that we were only going through, he nodded and slowly followed with that "crazy lady" look in his eyes. What was my supervisor thinking? Seeing the humor in any situation is another life skill I have always embraced. Learn to laugh at yourself – or someone else will.

I have heard of school psychologists who use a broom closet. Yes, any small space with a table or desk will do. We usually carry our materials with us. We are an adaptable profession. In my early years, I was very lonely and never really knew whether I was doing the job the way it was intended to be carried out. I spent some slow days mostly hiding out in my office and waiting for someone to tell me what to do. My employer called mandatory meetings once a year but that was the only limited contact I had with other school psychologists. I did have required supervision meetings but those were few and far between and none of the other school psychologists knew my school, so feedback was minimal. I was basically a tester in those early years and held meetings with teachers and parents and imparted my words of wisdom in the best way I knew how. I thought I was very skilled, but in retrospect, my skill was from textbooks and limited by my lack of hands-on experience with children. Some school psychologists remain in this limited role their entire careers and are comfortable with that.

In private schools, school psychologists were, until recently, housed in mobile units. I have always worked in private schools, usually with a religious affiliation. I am very comfortable in that setting since it is where I spent a great deal of my life. I became very familiar with mobile units over the course of my career. They are essentially trailers that house "government employees" who are mandated by state laws about special education. It used to be that these employees were housed separately from the private school personnel due to laws regarding the separation of church and state. These laws have since changed in some states. Although there are other people typically working in these mobile units, most look to you – the school psychologist for advice, and this can be daunting when you are just getting your feet wet. You often feel isolated by the nature of the job as well as the physical distance from the school and the population you serve. When you work in a private school, you spend a significant portion of the school day walking from the school to the mobile unit. The plus side is that if you are a competent school psychologist and stay involved, there is no need for a health club to stay physically fit. Yes, I definitely had an easier time than most working off those pregnancy pounds.

In my early years as a school psychologist I mostly received referrals from teachers and principals and conducted evaluations with students that were having academic and/or behavioral difficulty. Back then, not much was done with these individual students in the regular classroom setting before they were referred to the school psychologist. These days, most schools know that many alternative approaches to teaching or interventions should be attempted with a student before a referral is made. An evaluation is really the last step in the process. That is not to say the teachers I worked with were clueless about what should or could be done and some may have tried things on their own, it was just not the accepted procedure. Class sizes were generally bigger and many were just overwhelmed with any student who stuck out as needing a lot of extra help or not making the expected gains in reading, writing or math for their age and grade placement.

An evaluation mainly consisted of an intelligence test, a test of achievement, a visual-motor screening and a speech/language screening. That along with the mandated observation was supposed to tell me all I needed to know about a student so I could make my "helpful" recommendations to the teacher and parents. Other than the fifteen to twenty minutes allotted for "establishing rapport" at the beginning of the first testing session, many school psychologists, myself included, spent little time actually getting to know the student they were asked to make life altering decisions about. Still, this is the way things were done, especially in schools that had a large student population and a school psychologist two days a week or less. There was just no time to do it any other way.

So, I spent much of my time talking to a teacher who had made a referral, evaluating the student, meeting with the parents and talking to the teacher again about what was "best for the student." I remember many times not even being sure myself if my recommendations were "best" for this particular student but that's what the books said, according to the scores I had derived. We tended to fit children into neat little categories like LD (Learning Disability), DH (Developmentally Handicapped), or Severe Behavior Handicap (SBH), depending on their scores on these "tests" that were administered over the course of maybe four to five hours and minimal observations. That was fine with me at the time. After all, I had gone to graduate school for this. I was a trained professional and I had the data to back up my label. Some of these conferences with parents were difficult for me but I knew it was my job to deliver the verdict.

"Sometimes they just have to hear it, even if they don't want to," my supervisor during internship had told me. "It's never easy to say a child is developmentally handicapped but they'll just have to face the facts. It is what it is." End of story. Do it and move on to the next one.

I do like to think that even during my early years in the profession, I was never this callous. I remember thinking, "How does one accept that news as a parent?" How do you move on from that and tailor your dreams and hopes for the future? It seemed very limiting. I was sure some parents would move past the label but others wouldn't and would define their child by whatever label I supplied in that thirty minute meeting. I realize now that the same can be said for the opposite label. The "gifted" label, in my opinion, can be as limiting to children and parents. I believe every child is gifted in some unique way. Maybe it isn't as obvious in some and you have to dig a little deeper to find it. Most children shine if you give them the chance and meet their needs. By labeling children as academically "gifted" we as parents and educators often define them and set them up for disappointment and heartache if they ever fall from that pedestal. Still, in my early career, after a few minutes of thinking about the label and reviewing my test results, I delivered the "findings", whatever they happened to be. It was my job and I was a professional in the true sense of the word. Professionals think uninformed people always care what they know. I have learned that the delivery and caring approach is the key. You can't impress an audience if you've never had their attention in the first place.

It was many years later before I would reflect on some of those earlier meetings I had with parents and realize that maybe I could have been more compassionate and delivered the inevitable blow in a kinder way. But, I only occupied one seat at that point – the school psychologist, the tester, the professional. Ultimately, the one who had all the knowledge and I, like so many professionals, thought that was enough. Although at times I would move around in that seat, trying to get comfortable with my role, it was the seat I was assigned and so I embraced it in the best way I knew at that moment in time. It was the only side of the table I had ever occupied.

I remember one case in particular where I had evaluated a boy in second grade who was having considerable difficulty in the "regular classroom." He wasn't reading where he should be, his writing was illegible and his overall intelligence was in question by the teacher and all who interacted with him.

After meeting with the boy over the course of a few weeks and observing his behavior once in the classroom and once on the playground – I had a label that fit him fine. He was Developmentally Handicapped (DH). Had to be, his IQ was under 70, and that's what the criteria in the "blue book" put out by the state said. He also exhibited weak adaptive behavior, which is another qualifying factor for the DH label. At that early stage in my career I failed to consider many of the other factors that could have been contributing to a low IQ score, including lack of memory skills, and poor auditory skills. In essence, many times a child's intelligence is really higher than traditional IQ scores show. But, I was strictly a textbook type of school psychologist at that point in my career. The textbook clearly said this child was Developmentally Handicapped. After conferring with the principal at the school and the child's teacher, we decided that a "special school" would be better suited to meet this child's needs. I had heard of this school, but had never been there in person myself. I made several phone calls and determined that there was a spot and the school was willing to take the boy mid year. After several conversations with the transfer school's principal and another school psychologist friend who was employed by the public school system as a liaison to private schools, I also found out more about this school. It seemed likely that this boy would be going to school with a vastly different population than his current school. Many of the students this new school served had multiple handicaps and physical limitations. Many were also much lower in intelligence than this student was. Nevertheless, he fit the category and so I ventured on in my quest to do what was "best" for the student. I met with the parents and explained to them the findings of my evaluation. I suggested that they visit this prospective school and see what opportunities it could provide for their son. They agreed to this but did ask several times if I had visited the school. I assured them, that I had not but had "heard some wonderful things about it." At the time I thought that was a ridiculous question. Why would I visit the school? I was just supposed to look at the data and make the recommendations. No one said anything about visiting the school. This is where we sent students like their son. That was enough for me.

I remember playing phone tag with the mom for several weeks after this. I had set up an appointment for them at the school. Had they gone? I wasn't sure but I got the distinct impression that the mother was avoiding me. I like to call this my "get a clue" phase as I had no idea why they were avoiding me. It was also over a holiday break so I wasn't sure if she was truly avoiding me or just out of town. After school resumed and I still didn't hear from the parents, I began to become concerned about the placement. We were on a deadline to enroll their child in the school, after all. Didn't they get that? There was paperwork to be done, after all. I had to wrap this up!

Finally, I heard from the principal. Apparently the parents had visited the proposed school and called her to request a meeting with myself, the teacher and the principal. I walked into that office confident that the parents loved the school and were ready to transfer their son. Yes, accolades were about to be thrown my way. And well deserved they were.

Even in those early years, I was adept at reading body language. When I walked into the principal's office, my hopes of accolades faded quickly. The parents sat at one side of the table slumping in their chairs and looking something just short of miserable. The principal glared at me with at least moderate distain. Cordial greetings were exchanged all around and then we began to discuss the new school they had visited the day before. The father was the first to speak as he demanded,

"How could you possibly think our son would fit in at that school? We realize he is slightly behind, but he is nothing like those kids."

Feeling justifiably defensive, but trying not to show it, I asked him to explain exactly what he objected to about the school.

"I'm not sure what you're talking about. Could you help me understand what you object to?" Yes, that sounded like something I had been trained to say. A nice intellectual response was called for.

The distraught father went on to explain that most of these kids obviously "did not have a lot going on in their heads."

I believe that is a direct quote, as it has stuck in my head for years, as much as I've tried to expel it. Up until that point I thought my perspective was the only one that counted.

He also said that "most of them were in wheelchairs or had walkers and could barely get around. Our son is nothing like that and we won't even consider him going to that school under any circumstances."

I sat there for what seemed like ten minutes but was probably only several, trying to process what this man had just dropped on me. How could the boy not be going? I had already submitted all of the paperwork to the local district for placement and everything had been approved. The parent's visiting the school was merely a formality and the last step in this process. I had determined this was the "best" placement for their son and the principal had reviewed my findings and agreed. Come to think of it, the special education teacher who had done some achievement testing also agreed. The deck was definitely stacked in my favor and I wasn't sure I wanted to deal again at this point in the game. If they changed the plan now, it could all come tumbling down and someone would look like a fool. I was smart enough to know that someone would be me. Before this meeting, the father had never even opened his mouth. Why was he being so vocal now? More importantly, why was he speaking out against something that obviously was in the best interests of his son? I was baffled. I was astounded. Mostly I was annoyed, angry and confused as to how to proceed. I must have missed this class in graduate school. How do you deal with parents who thought they could change the game plan? That was definitely not in my limited handbook of school psychology wisdom.

As I sat there digesting all of this, the frustrated father inquired, "Why didn't you at least visit the place before you sent us there?"

I rolled this question around in my head and came up with some plausible explanation I do not remember to this day. I'm sure it consisted of some questionable excuses about being busy, not being able to schedule an appointment, etc. None of these seem even reasonably adequate today, but at that time they were how I rationalized my lack of forethought. All I knew then was that it did not seem the least bit important to me to visit that school. You see, I wasn't a parent, wasn't sure I would ever be a parent and frankly, could not relate to what these parents were going through. It seemed as simple as a "change in placement" to me. Yes, that's the box I had checked on the form, no big deal. Intellectually sound. Yes, all my ducks were in a row, so to speak. Or maybe all my "desks" would be a better metaphor.

In the end the boy ended up leaving the school anyway and going to another public school system. I think the story was that he was going to live with his grandmother so he could get better services in another system. I heard that the parents had talked to someone in a neighboring district and had been promised a special education category with a more acceptable name and better services in a "regular" building. The bottom line was that our school was not the right place for him. I knew that, and so I really didn't think much about the placement falling through. The principal and teacher seemed satisfied with the fact that he would no longer be their problem. That may sound callous or unfeeling but the bottom line is many teachers and administrators in private schools are overworked and underpaid and some just want the problem to go away. However this could be accomplished was fine with them. I'm sure we all believed that he might be better served in another setting as well. By the time this student had been referred to me, his academic issues coupled with unusual behaviors made making friends difficult. A new setting with better services might give him a fresh start. That's called rationalization in psychology. I chose to believe the student was better off. Actually, I don't think it was until years later when I even took the time to rationalize this. I was too busy thinking that I was justified in my recommendations for this student. This family's emotional adjustment to leaving a place they considered "home" never entered my mind. It was their problem, not mine.

Chapter 2

Maybe Another Year Will Do It?

Another common area most school psychologists are asked to weigh in on is retention. Retention is rarely recommended today but in the early years of my career, well-meaning teachers and administrators were readily recommending it for students who were struggling in acquiring reading in kindergarten or first grade. Typically I was asked to collect some data on the child in question to see if retention would be a logical step to recommend to the parents. An individual achievement test comparing the student's current level of reading, math and written language with his/her peers was usually where I started. Then I'd collect developmental information and behavioral samples from observations. All of this in hand, a meeting would be set up with the parents to go over all of this and address the idea of retention. As any seasoned person in education knows, this must all be mentioned by February and typically there is a log of conversations with parents before that. Most parents should at least be aware that their student has been struggling before this topic is ever addressed.

I distinctly remember one case involving retention I was asked to consult on. This was probably after I had been a school psychologist for about three years. The boy was in second grade, was young for his class (summer birthday) and was struggling a great deal with reading. His first grade teacher had given him a lot of individualized help as was his second grade teacher. He was receiving Basic Skills (small group intervention) in reading for the first half of the school year when he came to my attention. His teacher was considering recommending retention to the parents and wanted to know if I could "evaluate the situation" and give my opinion.

Well, I saw this boy for a total of about three hours, broken up into two different sessions. As I recall, I did some achievement tests which showed his reading skills were at the level of a beginning kindergartner. He was in the middle of first grade at this point so that was very low considering he had been given a lot of small group help. The boy also demonstrated immaturity in other ways on assessment instruments such as the "Draw a Person Test" and behavioral observations. Some things I noted were his difficulty with fine motor skills – holding a pencil and forming letters, drawing shapes and using snaps and buttons. He also had immature speech in casual conversation and word finding difficulties (language). He was also physically small compared to his classmates. All of these factors taken together made the boy appear to be functioning more like a first grader than a second grader. So, I concurred with the teacher that he was a good candidate for retention. The fact that he had a July birthday and was six to eight months younger than many of his classmates was the icing on the cake. The success rate for boys with summer birthdays in today's fast-paced schools is low unless they have exceptional academic skills.

With this recommendation in mind, we scheduled a conference with the student's parents, the classroom teacher, the principal and me. In most school settings where I've worked, the principal is present at conferences where retention is recommended. After presenting the parents with all of our information about their son, I stated that "all the data points to the fact that retention may be a good solution for your son." Well, the parents, understandably so, said they wanted to think about it for a week or so. They did realize their son had problems but were not convinced retention was the way to go. They understood our reasoning they said but were not sure about the social implications or the effect it would have on his self-esteem. I was well prepared with my standard response to that.

"Oh, kids at this age forget about this kind of thing very quickly. His classmates will hardly remember a year or two from now. The academic gains will be well worth any negative effects, I assure you."

All this wisdom was based on having read it in a book somewhere, and really believing it at that moment. I have always been honest with parents about what I know and believe to be true.

Well, I did hear from the parents a few weeks later and they said they had decided to have an outside evaluation done with their son. They were interested in a second opinion about the whole retention issue. This would probably take four to six weeks to complete and provide the school with a report. Fine, I thought – that will only prove our case. Every parent is entitled to a second opinion. That's what the books say, anyway.

At that point in my career, I was somewhat naïve about second opinions on the educational front. In reality most second opinions in education do not take into account how the student functions in the educational setting at all. Most of these opinions are gleaned from doctors or psychologists in private practice who administer some random tests and don't have any input on the child's performance from the school they are attending. They see the child for maybe two or three hours and do "observations" of the child's behavior in that limited setting. This, in my opinion, leaves a huge part of the puzzle missing. Many parents do not realize that they are really getting a medical perspective, not an educational one. Most seasoned educators know that a student generally acts much differently in a classroom of peers than in a waiting room or in a doctor's office with the parent. The conditions are just not the same and any decisions made on this basis are skewed, to say the least. Many medical professionals, while well intentioned, are unaware of the realities of an educational setting. So, unless the private practitioner has sought out observations from a variety of people in the educational and home settings, and ideally done an observation themselves in these settings, I am skeptical about the validity of "second opinions." Yes, I like my puzzles completely filled in, not with gaping holes that make me wonder where that last piece is.

After about five weeks or so, I was beginning to get anxious about this whole situation. It was getting close to April and probably some decision needed to be made soon. After checking with the classroom teacher and the principal, they suggested that I phone the mother and see if they had any results yet. When I did finally get in touch with the mother after playing phone tag for a week she said that yes, the results were in and I should arrange a meeting at the school. Well, fine, I thought. Were you planning on calling us or not? I have other cases to work on and this one really needs to be resolved. That was clearly my egotistical period. It was all about me and closure. That's when I was naïve enough to believe closure really existed. Now I know it is an overused word and rarely lives up to its reputation.

The meeting was scheduled for the next week in the principal's office. The players were all present – the doting parents, the worried teacher, the stern administrator and the well-informed school psychologist. Yes, categorizing people was in the job description back then. I've come to realize that in reality it serves no one, least of all a student. People do not fit into nice neat boxes. The parents presented us with a report from a well-known psychologist in the area. This woman was actually nationally known and had a newspaper column too, so I was impressed with their ability to obtain an evaluation from her. The meeting was short. The parents basically informed us that it was this woman's professional opinion that retention would not benefit their son and we could read the report over at our leisure and call them if we had questions or wanted to meet again. Bottom line – they would not be retaining their son.

Well, I did read over the report in the next few days. This psychologist had done some similar testing to what I had done. Some achievement tests, some tests of maturity and a variety of observations of the student in different settings. She also had done quite a bit of research on retention and the pros and cons of it for students. She had some impressive data on the percentages of retained students who showed little benefit from repeating a year in the early grades. She also cited several studies that demonstrated that there is actually a negative effect on the self – esteem of children when they are asked to repeat. The negative effect of retention outweighed any positive benefit. I thought it was a very thorough report overall and thought it interesting that this professional had taken the time to research the whole retention issue in such detail and provide the parents with that information.

Of course over the next year or so I monitored that student's progress, wondering if the parents had made the right decision. The boy did continue to struggle in third and fourth grade and then I basically lost track of him. In the field of school psychology, as in most professions, I'm sure, issues take center stage for a while and then other things come up and life goes on. The more important question that kept nagging away at me for a few years was, "Would he have struggled as much if he had repeated second grade?" I guess we'll never know. But either way, as the detached professional, it didn't affect my life much. Next case, please.

I did the best I could do as a professional in those beginning years, but I was not personally invested in most of the students I worked with. My training had prepared me well for the clinical expertise and data I needed to be adequate at my assigned tasks. It was not until years later when I would realize that training and expertise are only important if people feel you are genuinely invested in their dilemma and care about the well being of their children. Without this connection, book knowledge is shallow and useless. People don't care what you know until they know you care. It is crucial to show that you care.

Chapter 3

The Beat Goes On

After a couple of years of getting my feet wet in school psychology, I met the man who would become my husband. Not an easy feat in the world of education. As any one who has spent any time in this female dominated profession knows, the pickings are slim when it comes to prospective husbands and even slimmer in private schools. Because of the low pay scale, most men trying to support a family find private schools to be less than ideal. The same holds true for single men trying to save for the prospective wife and family, a car, house or any number of other material possessions. Of course there are always a few single men who do end up in private schools out of a deep sense of faith, a commitment to a cause or lack of other job offers, but I have never found the dating pool to be worthwhile.

Throughout my mid twenties I had toyed with the idea of getting married. Yes, it was something I definitely saw in my future. I just wasn't sure how to obtain it. So I went on a few blind dates, went on a few group dates and finally met a man five years older than me who seemed like "a good catch." Or at least someone I wouldn't throw back right away like I had done several times before. After dating for several months he asked me to marry him and thus began the saga so many women face of holding down a full time job and planning "the most important day of your life." That's what all the books say anyway. I must admit that I never got all caught up in the hoopla of weddings like some people do. I guess maybe I'm too sensible or didn't have the endless mounds of cash. I've really always thought it was more about the actual marriage than the one day event. So, while planning the wedding did take some of the focus off of my career for a few months, I'm sure I didn't agonize over every minute detail like so many brides do. It was just the ceremony after all. I knew I'd give more attention to the long haul. The main goal – meeting a man who I knew I could spend the rest of my life with and raise that wonderful Brady Bunch style family – had been accomplished!

It was during the third year of my school psychology career that I went from being a Miss to a Mrs. Since the wedding was to take place at the end of September I started out the year with my new married name. I was beginning in a new school and thought that would simplify matters rather than having faculty and students learn my maiden name just to have to switch it in a few short weeks. Since my maiden name and my new married name both began with "Sh" this seemed even more logical. If nothing else, I've always been logical. Of course this did cause some unexpected confusion I had not anticipated.

The first day at my new school in August, I explained to the principal, who was a middle aged woman, my decision to go by my married name, since the wedding was only a month away. She seemed to understand and shook her head profusely. She then proceeded to take me around to the different classrooms and introduce me to the faculty who were getting their rooms ready for the opening day of school. The first few introductions went fine.

"This is Mrs. Mary Shafer, our new school psychologist."

This followed by a few comments about my impending wedding date, my background, welcome, blah, blah, blah. Midway through the faculty introductions her mind must have wandered and she began introducing me by my maiden name.

"This is Mary Schomisch, our new school psychologist."

When I realized what was happening, I tried to stop her and gently point out the error of her ways but she was on a roll and was a woman with a mission. Apparently she was in a hurry to get all the introductions done and get on with the business of preparing the school for opening day. I fully understood this at the time and thought it was really no big deal and it would all work out. That's me – the eternal optimist.

I should have known I was in trouble right away the next day. As I walked down the hall bright and early with all my pretty new pencils and shinny stopwatch, I heard.

"Good Morning Mrs. Shafer."

Of course that didn't grab my attention in the least. They must have been talking to someone else. "Shafer" – that sounds familiar anyway. I know that name from somewhere. A few minutes later, as I crossed the street approaching the mobile unit in the distance another teacher said,

"Oh, you're Miss Schomisch, the new school psychologist, aren't you?"

"Yes, that's me, how are you doing this morning?"

It wasn't until I was sitting snug in my new "office" in the mobile unit that I remembered. Oh, my gosh, Shafer, that's going to be my last name! She was talking to me!

This was only the beginning of the name game confusion I was to endure for the next several weeks. Half of the school lists had my name as "Schomisch" and half as "Shafer". Half of the faculty thought the new school psychologist was Miss Schomisch and the other half Mrs. Shafer. Of course it would probably be more accurate to say a third each way since to this day some faculties still probably don't know who their school psychologist is. Yes, I have come to find out it is one of those well kept secrets in certain schools. There will undoubtedly always be administrators and teachers who refuse to accept the fact that they might need a different perspective in an area where they lack training. Thus school psychology remains an underused profession in some arenas. That, in my opinion, is a disservice to students and families.

Yes, it took a while for teachers, students and parents alike to determine that Miss Schomisch and Mrs. Shafer were in fact the same person. I had people who had only met me briefly approach me and ask me who I was. When I commented, "I'm Mrs. Shafer," they would hesitate and say, "Oh, I'm looking for Miss Schomisch, the school psychologist." It was becoming increasingly clear that what started out as an attempt for me to simplify things in the end was wreaking havoc. The only saving grace was the fact that I only had to put up with this for a few short weeks. Soon Miss Schomisch would go away on a two week cruise, get lost at sea and only Mrs. Shafer would return. Yes, bring on the wedding!

After the wedding, things began to settle down in my world and I began to feel comfortable in my new role as wife and my semi-new role as school psychologist. I was actually assigned to two different schools that year and both kept me fairly busy. Both were fairly small elementary schools but they were close in proximity to our new house so traveling was easy. As anyone knows who has worked at several schools at a time, sometimes getting to the right place on the right day is half the battle. One year I worked at three different schools in a five day week. Several times in the beginning I'd drive into the parking lot, go into the mobile just to have a co-worker stare at me blankly.

"Isn't today Monday? Why are you here? You're usually here on Tuesdays, aren't you?"

About that time, turning three shades of red, I'd high tail it out to my other school, which inevitably was a forty minute drive. As is Murphy's Law, when these things happen, it's always the school that is furthest away that you are expected to make a bee line for.

Most of the referrals at both of my schools consisted of evaluations for learning issues. Although there is the rare exception, by the time most students are referred to the school psychologist they are struggling miserably. Someone is usually looking for a life-line and in most cases it is the classroom teacher. In rare circumstances it may be a parent. Typically this type of referral involves three to four hours of evaluation, a couple of meetings with parents and teachers and maybe an Individualized Educational Plan (IEP) meeting if the student qualifies for special education. In the beginning I found this whole process to be fairly exciting and was eager to work with each student who was referred to me. As my years in the field increased, my ultimate goal was to keep each referral as new and fresh as those first few, but we all know that after years in any profession the same old thing becomes routine and thus sometimes I felt like I was just going through the motions.

I was also referred some students for counseling in those early years. As part of the school psychology training program

I had chosen a concentration in Counseling and Consultation. I had hoped to use this knowledge at some point in the schools I was employed in but had been informed that the bulk of my work would be "testing." Over the years I have come to enjoy the counseling part of the role greatly but often wish I had taken more hands on classes. Counseling is one of those areas where you hope you are making a difference. I have had students in counseling for six to eight weeks working on a particular problem, like aggressive behavior. They learn the proposed techniques, use them and then seemingly forget them the minute they leave counseling and are back in the real world. This used to baffle me in the early years when I guess I actually thought I had the power to cure these disruptive tendencies.

I remember right after I returned from wedded bliss being referred two brothers who were both have issues dealing with their parents impending separation. They were in fourth and fifth grades and although the mom inquired whether I would be able to see them together, I thought it better that I see them individually. I remember setting up the times with their teachers and having a vague idea of some things I could work on with each of them. That's about as far as my planning went.

Anyone who has even vaguely called themselves a counselor knows that the thirty or forty-five minute session can drag on into forever if you don't have a set agenda. I found this out quickly. After meeting the fourth grader the first time at his classroom at the scheduled time, I decided to start with the "building rapport" phase, as psychologists like to call it. This is basically the get-to-know each other part that is so crucial if anything really meaningful is going to be accomplished. As I found out immediately, this ten year old boy had not read the same textbook that I had. I was trying to make small talk and he was doing what ten year-old boys do so well – looking at the floor and avoiding all eye-contact. Suddenly it hit me – paper and crayons – that's what we need. Amazingly, that did seem to do the trick and soon he was at least uttering short, succinct information about his family and background. Yes, we were on a roll. I thought I even saw a smile starting to emerge at one point. Feeling like I was making real headway and it must be time to take this young lad back to his scholarly pursuits, I glanced at my watch. What? My watch must have stopped. I still have twenty minutes left? Why isn't this as much fun as it promised to be in the training? Somehow I managed to find a "feelings game" in the overstuffed cupboard and we played that until our first session finally came to an end. Needless to say, I was better prepared for the next session.

Although I have seen siblings in counseling several times since then, it is always an interesting scenario. Sometimes siblings can be almost exact replicas of each other. There are other times when I am truly amazed that the same woman gave birth to the two individuals I see on a weekly basis. It is also somewhat surprising that siblings raised in the same environment and experiencing the same circumstances, such as divorce, respond to it in a totally different way. You never know quite what to expect when dealing with siblings in counseling. I have come to realize that this is exactly the point. The best approach is probably not to expect anything. Any preconceived notion of how they will or should act based on their sibling is probably short-changing both individuals.

Most school psychologists also conduct some counseling groups if time permits in their schedule. I always enjoy presenting ideas to principals when I see a need and more often than not they are responsive if the idea is presented in a meaningful way. This, of course, can also be a challenge if it isn't well-planned. The first group I ran like this was for sixth grade girls who were basically getting in fights all the time and wreaking havoc on the educational environment. The principal asked if I would be willing to run a "social skills" group. Sure, why not? Sounds simple enough and of course I am up for the challenge, being the eager beaver school psychologist I am. Fourteen twelve-year-olds in a room for thirty minutes – no problem. Think again. Did I mention that I was somewhat naïve and optimistic the first few years I was a school psychologist?

The first problem with doing any type of a group with middle school students is that most of them don't want to participate in the first place. Typically they are told they have to participate or are strongly coerced by their teacher or parents. Think prisoners shackled to each other on the chain gang and you might get the idea. The second problem that I did not foresee is the noise level. I have never taken a group of more than eight girls since that time. Even if they are well-behaved, which is never the case if they are referred for "social skills", the sheer volume makes the room loud. It is difficult, if not impossible, to find a room in a school where it is permissible to be loud. It is also generally not a good advertisement for social skills training if the people walking past in the hallway need earplugs to muffle the volume.

Although I did have a fairly comprehensive social skills program lined up when I agreed to take on this group, keeping fourteen girls invested in changing their behavior on a weekly basis is challenging, to say the least. Many of the lessons I had planned were mocked and ridiculed on a weekly basis. Yes, you have to toughen up real quickly when you are a fresh, right off the rack, newbie school psychologist. I learned really quickly to be firmer than I would have liked if we were ever going to get anything accomplished. I am a firm believer in not wasting time that could be spent doing something else productive. If these girls were going to spend thirty minutes a week with me, then it was going to be time well-spent even if I had to put on my stern face to accomplish that. It was gratifying in the end to see that once I established the rules of the group and outlined specifically what was and wasn't acceptable, most of the girls respected that and I had few problems thereafter. I learned that it is important when running groups with children to establish clear guidelines of acceptable behavior and ramifications if the guidelines are not followed.

Chapter 4

Let the Games Begin

We decided to start trying to have a family within the first six months of getting married. I was almost thirty and he was thirty-five so we thought since we both wanted kids, we'd better start trying. Well, as luck would have it, I got pregnant almost instantaneously. I was thrilled and began making all the baby plans I had dreamed of. Well, things rolled right along and within three years we had two beautiful children. I was busy, busy – still working part-time and taking the kids to in-home day care.

When you are in education and begin to have kids of your own, the whole school setting takes on a different meaning. Everywhere I turned there were parents making decisions about their children and I knew that soon, I too, would be faced with many of these life-altering decisions. Where should the kids go to school? Should it be public or private, small or large? Yes, they were only two and three and I was already pondering the choices on the horizon. These were some many questions running around in my postpartum brain. I've never considered myself to be someone who would consider putting my kids on a waiting list for preschool when they were in the womb, like some of my neighbors were doing, but I knew our local preschools filled up fast. On the other hand, the good thing about having your first two children eleven months apart like mine is that they always have a playmate close to them developmentally. I actually think this spurred my son, the younger of the two, on in many developmental areas. He read at age four and a half, because his sister was reading. This is unusual for boys. To this day he has an extensive vocabulary and a love of knowledge that undoubtedly had its roots in those early years.

When my daughter turned three, I began researching preschools. I did not necessarily want her to attend a three year old preschool, but knew she would go when she was four. I actually inadvertently found out I had missed the cut-off for registering for three year old preschool anyway. By the time I decided to start looking it was April or May after she turned three and several people at the schools I visited looked at me in utter dismay and exclaimed,

"Well, you don't have a chance of getting her in next year. We've had a waiting list for six months already."

After explaining that I was really interested in the four year old programs, they looked astounded.

"She won't be going to three year old preschool? That's too bad."

You'd think I had just said I was selling her to natives in the Amazon valley or something. I really didn't think it was "too bad" until people began to label it that way. Actually I've never thought three year old preschool was much more than glorified babysitting and I have viewed it as not all that worthwhile for children who have a stimulating home environment. On the contrary, I think it is crucial for children who live in impoverished areas and need the early readiness skills it provides.

Of course, as is the way with many decisions in my life, this bit of wisdom came back to haunt me later. When my daughter started preschool in the fall of 1995, she was one of two "new" students in the four-year-old class at our local parish school. I thought this distinction rather odd from the get-go since it was a brand new year and every student was new to the four year old curriculum. It was a different room, different teacher and new, different toys as far as I could tell. The idea that she would be new never occurred to me. On the first day, I dropped her off with her bright, shiny new lunch box, the dress I had wrestled her into and her new crayons. I distinctly remember her barely turning to wave good-bye to dear old mom. She has always been an independent, hoopla-free type of child. Knowing what I know about separation problems and not wanting to tamper with perfect good-byes I counted my blessings and left quietly. As I departed I silently thanked God that I wasn't the mom with the small cling-on resembling a boy.

When I returned that short two and a half hours later my little girl growled at me as she jumped in her car seat.

"I was one of the new ones in the class, Mom. Why didn't I get to go there last year like everyone else?"

I've never been big on labeling children, so this bothered me, more than I let on. After the initial shock of her being branded as new wore off, I explained to her the reason.

"You see honey, you aren't really new, all of the four year olds are new to that class. Some of them may have gone to the three year old class last year, but that's a whole different program – totally separate."

That should take care of that, I thought, case closed. As I resumed my driving and tried to block out the screams of a three year old temper tantrum in the back seat, I heard a firm, insistent voice ask.

"But why, Mom, why couldn't I go?"

The stubborn daughter I've come to accept nineteen years later, making her premier. By this time we were pulling into our driveway so I shut off the car, turned around and prepped myself for the long version of my beliefs about preschool.

"Look, it's like this. Some people think their kids need to go to three year old preschool to learn to play, color and get along with other kids. I don't think that is true, especially when you have a brother so close to your age. You and he get along wonderfully, you learn a lot, and I am home with you most days, which some mom's aren't. That's all I can tell you. Do you understand?"

"I guess so, but I still wish I had gone so I wouldn't be new."

So much for my well-delivered speech on the merits of preschool.

After her second day of preschool she was all smiles when I picked her up from school.

"How'd it go today?" I inquired.

"Oh, I had lots of fun", she said, "We painted some pictures and read some books and went to the dress-up corner. The best part was what happened when one boy called me the new kid again."

"What happened?" I innocently inquired, hoping she hadn't punched him.

"I told him what you said about not everyone needs to go to three year old preschool and I just didn't need to go. Maybe he and the rest of the kids did – but I didn't, because I have a brother. I told my teacher too and she listened real close."

Wonderful, I thought. Now my daughter was teaching the teacher – with a little help from know-it-all mom, of course.

That occasion marked the first time I would impress a teacher with my infinite wisdom, but undoubtedly not the last. As the years went on I learned a thing or two and tried to stifle my opinions around the kids. I also cautioned my children about sharing educational wisdom they picked up at home. Yes sharing in the younger grades should probably be confined to show and tell. I pride myself on being a quick study.

The next year when my son started preschool and my daughter full day kindergarten, I was already in the groove of school. Everything seemed to go a little smoother. He was not labeled the new kid. Luckily for me, he had the same teacher, so it wasn't necessary for him to impart any of my vast wisdom upon her. She obviously was a quick study on the whole preschool issue too. He loved preschool as my daughter had but we did have issues with his wardrobe. For some unknown reason my oldest son enjoyed dressing up when he was younger. He always wanted to wear nice shirts, pants and sweaters to preschool. As anyone who has spent anytime around young children knows, this is counterproductive to the messy curriculum that is a part of the preschool experience. I knew this would be a problem from day one of preschool. After explaining to him how "it would be better to wear something not so nice to school and save those fancy clothes for church" he nodded in agreement. Imagine my surprise then when the jeans and t-shirt he had picked out for the first day ended up in a ball on his closet floor. As I called to him that it was time to leave for school he appeared looking like he was ready for a formal wedding, not a day of finger painting and modeling clay. Grey wool slacks, dress shoes, button down white shirt and clip on tie.

"Can I wear my sport coat too?"

After the initial shock wore off I responded, "No, and what happened to the jeans you set out last night?"

"I really want to wear this Mom. I like to look handsome. It is the first day."

For someone who has always impressed upon my children the importance of neatness and first impressions, I found that difficult to argue with on the first day. So, as we walked out the door to my little man's first day of preschool, I felt a hint of pride in my son mixed with sheer pity for that poor unsuspecting teacher who was destined to deal with another of my strong-willed offspring. Not to mention the know-it-all mom who came along for the ride.

My daughter's kindergarten experience got off to a wonderful start. I was thrilled that our local parish school had all day kindergarten, as I have always been a strong believer in that for most kids. I know people who still believe half day is fine but in my experience that is usually more about mom resisting letting the child grow up. I knew after two and a half hours of preschool four days a week my children would be ready for all day enrichment and frankly, I was ready for them to be educated by someone besides me. For this reason I have never been a big believer in the whole home-schooling philosophy. I am realistic enough to know that I need to be away from them for a portion of the day, and likewise they benefit from being away from me. Full day kindergarten was one of the criteria for picking a school and on that one, I wasn't about to compromise. By the time my second was two years old I was also pregnant again which certainly figured into the equation. I was confident my two oldest would get more enrichment at school all day than at home with mom and a younger sibling who required a lot of attention. I know people who supposedly home school five children when they have two or three others under the age of four. How this works, I'll never understand. Seems to me like the ratio for in-home day care is stricter than the ratio for home-schooling your own children. Yes, we are a nation of inconsistency in regulations.

My oldest learned to read by the end of kindergarten. All on her own really. I don't believe in forcing children to do anything until they are developmentally ready. I've never been one to sit around with other moms and brag about what my child could do at any stage of the game. The growth and development of children just does not seem like a contest to me. Perhaps it's unintentional, but some people seem to make everything a contest. "My child was potty trained at a year and a half." Good for you, but I don't think it will guarantee them success as an adult. I never saw that on a job application, "Please list when you were potty trained." Or "What age were you when you began to read?" In the big scheme of things, these milestones are not all that important, but in our competitive society, moms like to compete as well as any group.

From the time she was about three years old, random people began to inquire whether my daughter could read. "Is she reading yet?" Even though I was in education and knew better, since she was my first, I seriously began to wonder if I should be worried. Although we had read to her off and on since she was an infant, mostly at three she was sitting on books that got in her way or chucking them across the room at her two-year-old brother. No, she was definitely not reading them. Of course my neighbor's daughter was reading, and to hear her mom talk, she was putting every other toddler to shame. Apparently the child prodigy had read through their Golden Books collection of ten Disney stories in a week. Bravo, bring on the band! Although this attitude can get under a new mom's skin, if you let it, I knew my oldest would read in her own time. People I hardly knew actually asked me, "Well, are you helping her along with alphabet letters and sounds? Surely you are trying to teach her to read?" When I replied, "No, she'll do it when she is ready, we have books all over the house" the looks were piercing. If I hadn't known what I did about development, I undoubtedly would have been consulting some reading program for her. This competitiveness among moms can take its toll and I began to shy away from play groups when I had my son. Besides the fact that he and his sister had each other to play with, I became frustrated with the competitive nature of the so called "adults" and the pressure they put on their children. Of course this only gets worse as children get older. I'm not sure if this attitude is unique to Americans or applies to the human species in general.

Of course when my eldest did begin to read, I was swelling with pride. It is something special when your first child begins to make friends with books. Maybe this is more of a milestone when you, as the parent, are an avid reader. I value reading and it has always been a companion to me. I remember growing up, our formal living room was hardly ever used. We four kids had strict instructions from mom and dad that it was for company and we were not to play in there. We were not allowed in at all except for reading. In retrospect I have wondered if this was my father's subtle way of encouraging us to read for pleasure. He was an encyclopedia salesman and had a love of knowledge. He also always had a way of subtly getting his message across. I think he was a psychologist before his time. The beautiful untouchable room became a place you could only enter if you had a book in your hand. I spent many lazy Sundays lying on the golden velvet couch with a good mystery or a romance novel. Yes, when I couldn't find a friend to hang out with, I could always find a book to lose myself in. So, I guess part of me hoped that books would be a good friend to my daughter as well. They have a way of teaching, inspiring and opening up new worlds to explore.

From the time my daughter began to read her brother became interested in books too. She would bring books home from the school library and they would sit on the couch and she would read them to her brother while I was fixing dinner or otherwise occupied. Reading inevitably brought them closer together. Up until that point they had always played well together but like any brother and sister so close in age, had their share of spats too. Reading gave them quiet time together and of course filled big sister with pride since she had a skill her brother did not. Maybe this was the beginning of their competitive nature which continues fifteen years later.

My son followed suit and a year later began to read midway through kindergarten. He was reading by the time he turned five years old in January of that year. I distinctly remember that it was six months earlier than my daughter read, but she insists that I am wrong and she read at a younger age. Did I mention that they are competitive? Actually, for a boy he hit all developmental milestones earlier than most. He was talking in full sentences by the time he was two and a half and has always had an extensive vocabulary. Friends who had boys at the same time would tell me that their sons were stringing two words together, while mine was talking in complete sentences. Of course I had the sense not to point this out for fear of becoming one of those competitive types or being stoned on the playground. I credit his achievement to the fact that he has a sister who is ten and a half months older than he. Of course a good gene pool never hurts but he followed big sister's lead on a lot of things. I used to remind her of this important fact. "He would not have read so early, if you were not around to show him how." This used to put a smile on her face when she was younger because somehow it still gave her the upper hand. Yes, that psychology degree was not wasted.

My eldest two progressed equally well through the primary grades. They were right on track with their peers and even ahead of their peers in some subjects. They both seemed to excel in school. They both liked school too. What more can a mom who happens to be a school psychologist ask for? Yes, all was right in my world.

Everything was running so smoothly that I decided to go back to work part-time after my new son, the third born was about a year old. I had previously worked part-time when the two others were toddlers but had decided to take some time off again after our third was born. The rationale for this was mainly an economic one. On the salary I was making, by the time I paid for childcare for three young children, my paycheck was hardly buying diapers and formula. That coupled with utter exhaustion from having solo childcare duty led me to believe I should put the career on hold. My husband was traveling Monday thru Friday most weeks and thus wasn't able to help with the kids.

I was more than eager to get back to work during the school year of 1995-1996. I had arranged to take the third child to the same in-home daycare provider I had used when the two eldest were toddlers. It was close to their school and I could pick him up at the end of the day easily. Because I was also in a school which dismissed at the same time as theirs, I had them bussed to my sitter's house and picked up all three of the kids there. Yes, all was arranged and I was ready to get back into the adult world. Of course I had close friends who stayed home questioning my sanity.

"Do you need to go back to work? If I were you, I would stay home when they are so little."

I guess that is the point. They were not me. I have always loved to work. It has little to do with financial gain for me. I need to be needed and valued. I am not claiming that some women don't find value in domestic bliss. I don't fault them for that. I however, have always found limited satisfaction in cooking, cleaning and packing lunches. I also whole heartedly believe that I am a better mother when I work outside my home. It provides me with an outlet that fills a basic need that my family does not fill. I also believe I have some expertise to provide to students, teachers and administrators. I have been told I am a valuable school psychologist and I embraced that label early on. I like being needed and appreciated by people outside of my family. I don't believe that it is selfish to work outside your home. I don't believe my children have suffered. Actually, I have been told they are very well-adjusted.

I believe in some situations it is selfish not to find an outlet for yourself. I have seen too many women who are overwrought, angry and resentful because they are "full-time homemakers." I believe many of us who work are better moms because of our outside interests. We are less stressed and make good use of what little time we have with our children. Summers have always been fun for me but I am always ready to go back to school when my kids do, and I know they are ready for me to go back too. Too much time with kids can make even the best mom frustrated, quick-tempered and resentful. I think most women would agree with me if they are being honest. Of course I have always lived in the best of both worlds. Part-time work and a school schedule is the best. I realize I might have a different view if I had to work full time, twelve months a year. I am realistic enough to know this is the situation for many people. I am also experienced enough to know that this is the reality they choose because of priorities and material possessions they "can't live without." Most of life is about choices and prioritizing. Choices always come with costs and benefits.

So, from the time our third child was a year old I worked part-time. Some years I worked three days, some years four, depending on the school availability. I mostly stayed in the same schools consecutively but over the course of my career I have worked in roughly ten to twelve schools and districts. I have always enjoyed it and worked with some wonderful, caring individuals who helped keep me sane, motivated and positive. I have had the pleasure of getting to know many fine educators and a few who probably should have gone to culinary school, business school or anything besides the school of education. I have always taken these people with a grain of salt and tried to live by the philosophy that everyone does the best with what they have in a given situation. That and "it's not always about me" have served me well in preserving my sanity.

Chapter 5

The Third Time's a Charm

From the time my third child, was born, he has been a charmer. He was the perfect baby. Slept well, ate well and was very even-tempered. That was a blessing since his older brother, had been anything but those things. Currently he is a teenager and people still tell me how pleasant he is to be around. "Pleasure to have in class" is something I read often on his report card. Actually, I am not surprised as he is truly a "pleasure to have in the family" too. He is the first of my kids to offer to help me with anything that needs to be done. He is out shoveling the walk before I know it is even snowing. He's the one I can count on to actually carry the clean clothes up the stairs rather than tripping over them and blaming me. I always remind him that he is in the same position in our family that I was in my family of origin. We are both the third born and maybe he is just destined to be helpful like I was. Maybe he is proof that birth order does mean something.

When he began preschool, I had been back to work part-time for four years and was expecting baby number four. I was tired, irritable and in retrospect maybe did not devote enough attention to helping him with all the preschool readiness skills I should have. I really wasn't very concerned about preschool since the older two were still excelling in school and I thought, of course, that he would also. His preschool teacher confirmed that he was pleasant and cooperative but he began

to have "difficulty with numbers and letters." Midway
through the year, I knew enough about reading readiness to
be concerned.

I delivered my fourth child and third boy in January of his
preschool year. Although we always had books around and I
encouraged reading among all my children, I still can't be
sure if the fourth child took something away from spending
time with my second son and preparing him for Kindergarten.
That's called unresolved guilt for those of you new to the field
of psychology. Of course, as any mother knows, a new baby
leaves you exhausted, stressed and drained even in the best of
circumstances. My husband was still traveling extensively
and I had three other children under the age of nine to take
care of, so I guess mine were not the best of circumstances. I
am just optimistic enough, however, to realize they were not
the desperate, financially strapped circumstances many
mothers deal with either. At the time, I remember people asking me.

"How do you do it with four children so young and your
husband gone five days a week?"

My honest reply was, "How do you not?" I really have always dealt with the hand I was given and gone "full steam
ahead." I know I have my mother and father to thank for that
life lesson. Sometimes we are truly powerless to change our
situation but we always have control over how we react to
that situation. I have always preferred to "Just Do It", as
Nike says. Sometimes thinking too much can get you in trouble.

In private schools, preschoolers preparing for kindergarten are given the Early Prevention of School Failure (EPSF)
assessment in March or April of their preschool year. The idea

is to determine their current strengths and weaknesses in seven major areas related to school success and achievement. If a student is identified as having several weak areas that might impede success in school, the parents are given ideas on how to improve these areas over the summer. This instrument then "prevents school failure" if used correctly. If a child has many weak areas, the school team may recommend to the parents that the child wait a year for kindergarten and participate in another year of preschool or enrichment activities. Being a school psychologist, I have been on the "team" administering this instrument and also the "mom" waiting nervously in the hallway to see how her offspring measures up. In reality, since I know every facet of this assessment, I could have drilled my children beforehand, thereby insuring their success, but I have never believed in this approach. I believe it is in my child's best interest to go in "cold turkey" like every other child in their class. After all, I have always been genuinely interested in whether they are ready for kindergarten and would not want to skew the results to get a false positive. I'm also honest enough to realize it would be unethical in some way and unfair – two things I have never been. That is not to say I haven't at least asked them to "draw a picture of a man" and "write your name" – two things that appear before the actual day. Hey, maybe I just wanted to see if they knew how. I didn't tell them how much it was worth or add detail or anything – honest! I actually have a friend who administered a whole section of the assessment to her son before he took the actual screening. I guess she was embarrassed when the results came home and it was noted that he said, "Hey, I've done this before. My mom has it at home." Maybe that cured me of any desire to "help" my children more than the average mom could.

Well, when my third was administered the EPSF prior to kindergarten, he performed well. I think there were a couple of areas where he was slightly weak, but nothing significant. He actually scored above expectancy for his age in three of the seven areas and at expectancy in one. The kindergarten teacher who reviewed the assessment with me was not concerned and so neither was I. He looked like a fine candidate for kindergarten. He has always been one of the oldest in his grade, having a late September birthday and I have always been glad I made the decision to start him in preschool a year after he technically could have started. He was also on the small side for his age which impacted my decision. My husband didn't necessarily agree with this decision since he too is a September birthday, started Kindergarten when he was barely five and has always done well in school. But, like many educational decisions in our family, he bowed to my expertise. Likewise, I bow to his expertise in Physics, Math and most Sciences since I recognized long ago that I will never win any awards in these areas.

The beginning of kindergarten was great. We had moved to a new house when he was in preschool and so my older two had attended kindergarten at our former parish. This was my first experience with kindergarten at this school but I felt very comfortable, having worked at this school years before and knowing many of the teachers. Actually when we decided to move, we zoned in on an area that would allow my children to attend this small private school. Out of the five to six schools I had worked at, up until that point, this was my favorite. The staff was competent, friendly and it had the "family" atmosphere I found lacking at our previous school. Mostly, I was thrilled with his kindergarten teacher as I felt very comfortable with her and knew he would also. He seemed to love kindergarten from the start. He came home smiling and full of stories about all the "neat" things they did each day.

By mid year, however, some of the same difficulties I had seen in preschool begin to emerge. He had "difficulty with rhymes", something his preschool teacher had also pointed out. He just did not understand rhyming words even though I had bought flash cards, read rhymes to him and worked on this skill often. He also had general difficulty picking up on word families and patterns. This was troubling to me since these things are crucial for reading readiness. I set up a conference several times with his teacher that spring. The comments were always the same. "Very cooperative, happy and gets along well with the other children. He does seem to have some difficulty with phonics, though, and is not progressing as I would like." With this report and concerns about readiness for first grade I contemplated having him evaluated by a school psychologist in our public school district. Even when children attend private schools, the public school district of residence is responsible for evaluating and identifying learning issues. However, when I brought up this idea with his teacher, she felt I should hold off until she completed her end of the year assessment of his skills. She assured me that this would give us both a better idea of his progress and readiness for first grade.

I set up a meeting with her in late April that year after the assessment was complete. The results were very favorable and seemed to indicate to both of us that he would be able to handle the first grade curriculum. Like the EPSF screening instrument, her results showed that he was performing above expectancy in several areas. His phonics and letter recognition were coming along fine, too, so my worries were put to rest. I respected her opinion greatly and thus I held off on any evaluation.

When he began first grade the following fall, I was confident he would be successful. His teacher was fairly new and young but seemed energetic and eager. I have found that sometimes in education the younger teachers are more enthusiastic and eager but obviously lack the experience a seasoned teacher brings. Many times it is a trade off for parents. Young and enthusiastic is wonderful if your child does not have needs that require presenting material in a new innovative way that isn't always outlined in the textbooks. Stepping outside the box is often necessary and something new teachers don't know how to do or are not willing to do. Seasoned teachers often have experience with different learners and have realized that not all children learn in the same textbook way. However, they can be less than enthusiastic, having done the job for so many years. Of course these rules of thumb are simplistic and don't apply to all teachers in either category.

Well, by mid-year of first grade his teacher began to be "concerned" about his lack of phonics skills. He was performing above average in all areas except reading. He was a "well-behaved, pleasant child" as his teachers had consistently told me. He received outstanding marks on his report card in every area except Reading/Phonics and Spelling, which, of course, is directly related to Reading. Most children who have difficulty with Reading also have difficulty with Spelling since they both require a good working knowledge of the rules of phonics. I began to receive weekly phone calls from this teacher about her "concerns" which is always unsettling. After working with my son quite a bit at home, I became more convinced that he might have the beginning signs of a Learning Disability, something I was very familiar with at this point.

I remember walking into that February conference feeling nervous and anxious. Up until this point all of the conferences at my children's schools had been a breeze. I always received glowing reports and walked in confident and self-assured. This was different. I had butterflies in my stomach and felt like I was walking into a mine field. I knew my son was having difficulty and wasn't sure how the school planned on handling this. As I sat down on the parent side of the table I felt like an actor without a script. I felt unprepared and longed to be on the other side with the professionals who knew what was coming. Yes, this "hot-seat" was unfamiliar and down right uncomfortable. After reviewing his latest report card with me and asking if I had any questions the teacher casually mentioned that "retention might be the best solution to his difficulties." What did she say? Retention? Did I hear that right? After, I shook my head to clear my ears and initial shock wore off I responded with,

"Retention? That was never even mentioned in kindergarten. He is doing well in everything but Reading. His report card doesn't support that at all."

I knew this teacher was inexperienced but logically, it did not make sense to me as a school psychologist. Wait a minute, reality check. I was the mother in this scenario, not the school psychologist. Where was the school psychologist anyway? Hadn't I been asked to sit in on numerous "difficult conferences" like this one over the years? Hadn't I been asked to supply data for the parents? Where was the data to support this life-altering suggestion? If the school psychologist couldn't attend, there should have been data from her to support this suggestion. Had they even thought to collect data? As a professional, I was baffled by the lack of forethought. As a mother, I was using every ounce of my energy to stifle the tears that were rising in the corners of my eyes. She went on to present her case for why retention "might be the solution to all his problems." I ended up thanking her for her time and flew out of the school, fighting to support myself on wobbly legs that were threatening to give way.

By the time I arrived at the refuge of my mini-van I was a wreck. Always one to keep a stiff upper lip, I looked around to make sure no one I knew was in the lot. I then proceeded to put my head on the steering wheel and sob uncontrollably for what seemed like hours. Years later, when I replayed this moment in my head (again and again), I realized that I sobbed for myself as much as for every parent I had dropped the word retention on in a callous, unfeeling way. I knew intellectually this young, naïve teacher was merely doing the job she had spent four years learning in college textbooks. I had acted the same way in several conferences years before. She knew no different and obviously it wasn't meant to be a personal sting. But sting it did. That simple three syllable word I had learned to utter so well over the course of my career stopped me in my tracks – "retention." It cut through my heart and pierced every ounce of my being. Not my son. Retained? Did I hear her right? It felt like a bad nightmare. Retention was for other people's kids – not mine. As I reluctantly pulled my head up from the steering wheel, grabbed the tissues and glanced around, the reality sunk in. Yes, it was real. I was in the school parking lot. Welcome to the other side of the table and the pain and anguish that accompany it. Welcome to being blindsided by well meaning professionals with textbook knowledge. Welcome to motherhood!

As difficult as it was, I pulled myself together, dried my tears and began to drive home, to my mother-in-law and kids. Of course throughout the ten minute drive my mind kept wandering back to that conference. Every time I thought of the word "retention" tears would flood my eyes. How could this be happening? I had read to him since the time he was a newborn. I had done what a "good" parent was supposed to do. This wasn't "fair." I began to go through a wide range of emotions. I felt like a huge disappointment, a failure, and mostly a "bad mom." I also felt angry, and betrayed by a school I loved. How could they be doing this to me? I trusted that place to teach him phonics and reading. How could they let me down? I blamed everyone and everything. I blamed my profession and the person assigned to that school for not being there when I needed them to act on a student's behalf. It was all different now – this was my student! A school psychologist was an advocate for students and parents and I needed an advocate. For a brief period, I even blamed my son. Maybe he should have read with me more when I asked him to, instead of running and hiding most nights. Maybe he should have played less and studied those phonics flashcards more. Although the school psychologist in me should have known better, the "mom" in me took over and began questioning every decision I had made about him since birth. Mostly, I just felt like I wanted to go back in time and "fix it." Deep down I've always been a fixer. I like solutions and answers. I don't like cloudiness or uncertainty. This whole mess felt very uncertain to me. Maybe retention would "fix" his difficulties. But maybe it wouldn't. Who knew? Even with all my fancy degrees and "expert" knowledge in the field, it seemed cloudy at best. The phrase "unfortunately no one has a crystal ball", which I had uttered so many times when giving my expert opinion to parents, came back to haunt me. I felt like anything but an expert in this situation. I felt confused, bewildered, ashamed and mostly overwrought with gut-wrenching pain. I had been blindsided by a moving train and was desperately waiting for someone to pick me up and put the pieces back together.

After I had given myself a few days to recoup from the collision and lick my wounds, I pulled myself off the ground and devised a plan. Yes, enough of the pity party, it was time to act. If there is one thing I know about myself after years of studying psychology it's that I am basically a Type A personality. I am a high achiever and a take charge type of person. I can't just sit around and feel sorry for myself for too long without trying to come up with a solution and working to solve whatever difficulty I am faced with. The only person who could figure this out was me. My son's future was dependent on my strength, not my emotional crumbling. This called for objectivity. Factual books are generally objective. When the rest of life seems cloudy, I rely on facts. Good, solid facts. I decided I would start with the library and collecting all the information I could gather from experts on retention. Although, as a school psychologist, I knew some of the basic information about retention, I felt like I needed and wanted to do a complete overhaul of the current literature. I also felt like the school would respect and acknowledge good, solid facts as opposed to the emotions of a confused parent. I would leave no stone unturned in my quest to do what was in the best interest of my son. I knew the school psychologist in me had to advocate for the mom whose emotions had thrown her into a tail spin. Yes, the time had come to capitalize on my professional skills and really work for what was bound to be my most heart-felt referral. I vowed to pursue an objective opinion and thoroughly weigh the pros and cons before making a decision that inevitably would affect my son's future. I tried to put the emotions on the back burner and approach this situation with the drive and determination I had used to conquer any of life's difficult situations.

When I arrived home from the library that evening with about fifteen books stacked high, I remember my kids looking at me bewildered. Although I have always been an avid reader, my usual take-home load was two or three books maximum. This was certainly out of character for mom. As they stared at me in confusion my typically quiet husband even felt the need to inquire, "A little light reading?" After depositing my load on the dining room table, I took him aside for a few minutes and explained the situation and the retention dilemma. He had been out of town when the bomb was initially dropped, and I hadn't informed him of what went on at the conference yet. When I finished summarizing the conference using my detached school psychologist tone he looked up and said,

"So what do you think we should do?"

The whole "we" in the question kind of threw me, since I had made every major decision concerning our children up until this point. Maybe by default, but all educational decisions typically fell to me and I must say I expected nothing less for this life-altering decision. He had always traveled a lot and he is also very reserved and quiet. Thus most discussions we have about our children are fairly one-sided. I think he would agree that everything he knows about children and education he learned from me. He has very little hands-on knowledge of children in general and very limited knowledge of development and curriculum. That's o.k. with me, since I have very limited knowledge of computers, which are his area of expertise. Yes, we know our strong areas and we tend to stick to them. It has served us well in our marriage. So, although the "we" was a nice sentiment, I knew in reality this all-important decision would fall to me. Yes, I was the one who held my son's future in my hands. I was the one he would inevitably thank or despise years from now when the crystal ball became reality.

After researching the retention question in great detail, I came to the conclusion that my son was not a good candidate. It also became apparent that, had his teacher known anything about retention and when it is recommended, she likewise would have come to this conclusion. It was obvious that no one at the school had done their homework. My son was older for his grade placement. All of the research points to retention as being beneficial when students are young for their class, particularly boys with summer birthdays. He was only struggling in Reading and Phonics. He was performing above average in all other areas. This suggests a possible Learning Disability – not a case for retention. Anyone who knows anything about learning issues in general knows that they continue to exist whether a child is retained or not. Learning Disabilities require specific interventions to correct those and teach a child differently. Thirdly, he did not demonstrate immaturity or lack of cooperation with adults, another indicator that retention might be warranted. The biggest drawback to me though was the negative impact on a child's self-esteem. All of the major studies I consulted said that "the negative effects on self-esteem do not justify the possible positive outcomes." Besides reading this from the experts I had seen firsthand proof of this in my own household. One of my other sons had a friend who was retained and parents and students alike never seemed to let him forget that. Years later whenever the boys name would come up someone would inevitably remind people, "He really should be in a higher grade." Many times I had seen this boy hang his head in shame or walk out of the room when the subject came up. I could not put my son through this same ordeal unless there was some wonderful benefit. It was clear there was not. Case closed, end of discussion.

Armed with this information, I decided to write a letter to the principal outlining why I did not feel my third was a candidate for retention and why we would be having him evaluated for a Learning Disability. I concluded with a statement saying that he would be going to second grade, if not at this school, elsewhere. The principal was very prompt in responding and said that "after discussing the situation with the classroom teacher, they mutually decided that that he would be placed in second grade." As a mother I was pleased, but as a school psychologist, I took this to mean that the teacher had recommended retention inappropriately and the principal knew it. Although I was thrilled it would work out well for us, I was also somewhat taken aback by the whole situation. I felt certain that, had I not been knowledgeable about retention, my son would have repeated first grade unnecessarily. Our situation would have a happy ending, but what about the other mothers whose children may have repeated because they trusted a teacher to know when retention was appropriate? Where was their school psychologist, who should have played the advocate role I had assumed for years? Why was she not being utilized at this school? My heart ached for uninformed mothers as well as their children who might face years of shame and embarrassment with very little if any educational gains. What was happening here was disturbing and I felt it with every ounce of my being. Something more should have been done before the word retention was ever brought up at that meeting. I felt that as a mother and I knew that as a school psychologist. I never blamed the teacher, I blamed the lack of support for teachers at this school. Slowly, but surely, my faith in this place I called home was unraveling. It was an unsettling feeling and one I would replay in the years ahead.

Chapter 6

Solutions 101

Because of my son's difficulties in Reading and Phonics I decided the best strategy would be to have him evaluated before he began second grade. I thought about having it done privately by a very reputable agency, but concluded that our school district of residence could do the same thing. After all, we were tax-paying citizens that only used the bussing from the district at this point. At that point the district of residence was responsible for evaluating any child suspected of having a disability even if they attended a private school. The laws have change recently to be the district where your child attends school. Again, I know all this because I am a school psychologist, I'm not sure it is common knowledge to most parents although school districts do advertise "child find" at different public places like libraries.

I called our local district that April to inquire about an evaluation for my son. I ended up speaking to the Director of Pupil Services, summarizing his difficulties and casually mentioned that I thought he had signs of a Learning Disability since I was a school psychologist myself. I have never considered myself to be bossy or arrogant. I basically try to treat other people how I want to be treated. But I do not believe in hiding information from people. I think they have the right to know that I know more about educational issues than the average mother they deal with daily. That having been said, I would like to think that any other mother could have gotten an appointment for her son as quickly as I did. The fact is, I'm not sure that is true. Sometimes when people know you know your rights, they bend-over backwards to make sure you will never have to assert them. That has been my experience, anyway. Even though I have benefited from this treatment, it saddens me some. I realize this is probably true in every field, not unique to education.

I was very careful about how I explained this situation to my son. He has always been very sensitive and somewhat anxious in new situations. This evaluation would take place at our local public elementary school. He would be meeting with their school psychologist and working for about two hours. I wanted to make sure he did not think it was a "test." To most young children, the word "test" implies there is a grade and you can pass or fail. That is not the case in educational evaluations. They include intelligence testing, achievement testing, a visual-motor screening and a language screening. Sometimes, if a child has behavior issues, then behavior rating scales will be distributed to teacher and parent also. This was not the case with my son. He has always been very well behaved and cooperative at school and home. The idea is just to provide more information about a student who is having difficulty. This helps school personnel to figure out how best to help the student improve and do better. It also shows if a student would qualify for a Learning Disability program or any other special education classes. A parent and/or examiner should also assure the child that the process does not imply that they are "stupid," only that they are having difficulty acquiring skills in the typical way they are presented. So with all my mom/school psychologist information in hand, I explained what would happen to my seven year old son.

As we approached the public school building on that Thursday in May, I realized that I was feeling uneasy and nervous about the whole process. How many times had I evaluated a student over the past seven years as a school psychologist? I knew all there was to know about what tests would be given, how they were scored, what might be recommended depending on those scores. Why was I so anxious? Clearly I was better off in this situation than the average mom. Then I realized with some hesitation that it was undoubtedly due to the fact that for the first time in this evaluation process I wasn't in the driver's seat. My son and I were clearly passengers. I wasn't sure I liked being a passenger. Have I mentioned that I like to be in control? As we opened the door to the school and I glanced down at the small boy clutching my hand, he smiled up at me in his sweet, innocent way. Just then we reached the office and the school psychologist introduced herself, took his hand and asked me to come back in two hours. Oh, yeah, this is the part where the mom leaves. As he was led away, he glanced back at me, smiled and said,

"See you later, Mom."

"Yeah, see you later."

Time to act mature, keep walking and don't look back. Well, when I arrived two hours later to pick him up he was all smiles.

"I really had fun, Mom. There was lots of neat stuff to do. It wasn't scary at all. You were right."

Glad to hear it. Now where can I get a sedative to deal with waiting for the next few weeks for the results? Yes, that's what it would be.

"Just a couple of weeks and I'll call you with the results."

That's what the perky school psychologist had promised. Unfortunately I knew that "just a couple of weeks" often turned into a month, especially at the end of the school year when caseloads tend to be heavy. I know that patience is a virtue. I value patience. I just have a hard time mustering any when the stakes are high. My son's future seemed like high stakes. "Just a couple of weeks" seemed like a life sentence.

True to her word, the school psychologist called me about two and a half weeks later. She had results and wanted to make an appointment to discuss them with me. Great, I thought. Do you have evening appointments? Let's see, it's 8:30. I can be there by 9:00. In reality, I would have to sweat it out a little longer. We made an appointment for a Friday afternoon the following week. Reluctantly, I braced myself for another week of uncertainty and nervousness.

When I met with the school psychologist the following week, she was all smiles.

"He is such a nice boy, and very bright."

Well, that's a nice note to start out on, I thought. Seems like she had paid attention in that class we all took in graduate school about building positive rapport with parents. Conversely, I had had several conferences about him in the last few years that began with "He has a hard time with..." This is disappointing and hurtful to most parents – including me. What ever happened to "if you can't find something nice to say, don't say anything?" It doesn't take someone in education to realize that every person has wonderful qualities worth noting. These qualities are worth sharing with parents who are undoubtedly anxious and worried when required to attend a parent/teacher conference. It doesn't take a psychologist to figure out that parents are much more accepting of "difficulties" in a child if they are assured that the teacher has taken the time to notice the good in their child as well. This sets them at ease, puts them in an accepting mood and ultimately makes them more receptive to discuss difficulties. So I, as the parent in this scenario, was thrilled that this professional took the time to point out the good in my child. A simple thing, but so appreciated by a nervous mom.

As she went over the evaluation I took note of her findings from both perspectives. As interested as I was in my son's results, I was also interested in her technique. Since this was the first time I had actually been on the other side of evaluation results being explained, I realized I was in a unique position to critique the whole process. Yes, I might be able to pick up some valuable pointers for the next parent I met with. I believe in teachable moments and this seemed like it might lend itself nicely to that. Overall, I thought her explanation was well thought out and accurate. Of course there were some times when I made mental notes. Never say that to a parent. Or, I should explain it that way too – that sounds good, concise without being condescending. Yes, life is about learning and I like to think I never let an opportunity for growth pass me by.

As it turned out, it the results of his IQ test suggested that he was in the very superior range of intelligence. He actually scored in the 98th percentile, meaning that only 2% of the population is more intelligent. As a school psychologist, that is impressive, but as a mom, that is thrilling, exciting and downright jump-for-joy wonderful! Not that I would have loved him any less if he wasn't intelligent, it just confirmed what I knew and sensed deep in my gut. The fact that he wasn't grasping phonics and reading was not a sign of being unintelligent. As a mom, I sensed this, but as an educator, I needed the data to support my theory. The achievement tests, true to what I suspected, did demonstrate a gap between intelligence and achievement. He had the classic signs of a Learning Disability. His IQ test showed that he is very visual and hands-on. He learns best when material is presented this way. His auditory skills were very weak. They were below the average range. That tells a school psychologist that he would have difficulty learning phonics and reading since they are highly auditory in nature. In other words, students have to hear the differences in sound patterns to understand phonics and transfer those skills to reading words. It became apparent that he was not hearing the patterns, which was impacting school. A different approach of teaching him was in order, not retention. That became abundantly clear to me and the school psychologist concurred. She suggested that he be placed in a Learning Disabilities Program. I took this opportunity to ask her professional opinion about retention.

"Are you kidding? You'd never retain someone who is old for his class placement with his ability. He'll catch up in no time. I'm sure you know that kids who have a high IQ benefit from LD programs at a faster rate than most."

Yes, I know that. The problem was convincing other people when I was the "mom" and the school psychologist at the school my son was attending seemed to be unavailable or at the very least not utilized in the best way.

After the school psychologist finished up, I left there with a report in hand and the reassurance that I had made the right decision about my son. A little objective data served to validate my opinion. Because I knew enough to advocate for my son, he would be o.k. With what I knew about Learning Disabilities, I knew we would have some battles, but I felt confident that in the end he would thrive. Because I had been his advocate and knew the right avenues, he would do fine. Contentment soon turned to professional uneasiness, though. What about all of the other mothers who didn't question teachers or ask for more data? Where was the school psychologist who should have been called in? The seeds of doubt about my children's educational setting were being planted. I desperately clung to the belief that the seeds would die before they began to grow. I am an optimist, after all.

Chapter 7

The Service Plan

After meeting with the school psychologist at the public school that spring, I immediately phoned the private school my son attended and informed them of the results which indicated a Learning Disability. I made arrangements for the appropriate steps to be taken so that he could be serviced in the fall of second grade. An Individualized Education Program (IEP) is used to address these needs in a public school system. In a private school it is referred to as a Service Plan and is less legally binding. The public school of residence has to offer to provide services for the identified handicapping condition (which they did) and then a parent denies services and says they prefer to go to the private school. Most private schools then take the public schools findings and put them on a plan to accommodate the child's needs called a Service Plan. In my experience, the effectiveness of Service Plans varies from school to school depending on the expertise of the person implementing them (LD teacher) and the school psychologist overseeing them. I have seen Service Plans that were every bit as effective as an IEP in a public school system and I have also seen Service Plans that were followed in a haphazard, ineffective way. Often private schools do not have the personnel to implement them consistently or regular education teachers feel they can ignore them. This is especially true if someone (usually the school psychologist) is not advocating for students on Service Plans and keeping tabs on their needs.

When I spoke to the principal at my son's school that spring, she assured me that they had just hired a new Learning Disabilities tutor and she would make sure she had him on her caseload for fall. The buzz word then was inclusion and apparently this new person was an expert in that. Inclusion basically means servicing students with special needs in the regular classroom as much as possible instead of pulling them out for individual instruction. This serves to decrease the stigma among kids and keep them with their peers as much as possible. Up until that point I didn't know much about inclusion but I was confident he would receive good services, since I knew my rights and the school was aware that I knew my rights.

During the summer after my third completed first grade, he attended a local enrichment program at a nearby college to build on reading and phonics. I found it on my own, not through the school. Again, I credit this to my professional life. I knew about this program because I have always advocated for children and searched things out for the families I worked with. Many parents often look for activities to maintain current skills in their children who struggle during the school year. Even "average" students loose a lot during the summer months, but kids who are already struggling really need summer enrichment and continuity to prepare them for the next grade level. It was a very affordable program run by the Graduate School of Education. They utilize graduate students in education to instruct struggling students in small groups in Reading and Phonics. There was a great deal of individualized attention which I knew would benefit him and prepare him for success in second grade in the fall. It was basically how the graduate school prepared their students to become teachers. It provided hands-on experience for the teachers, also benefiting struggling grade school students. There was one teacher to every two-three students, which is a really good ratio.

Although he fought me every step of the way when I told him about the program he learned to enjoy it about a month into the summer. They had puppet theatre for the kids, trips to the library and other fun activities that worked on reading in subtle ways and incorporated the beautiful outdoors and fun. Most people think of summer enrichment programs as being indoors, stuffy and rote. This was anything but, and turned out to be a very enjoyable experience for him and mom. By the end of the summer he was actually starting to enjoy reading. "Enjoy" may be too strong of a word. Suffice it to say the he didn't run and hide when I mentioned "reading for a while." I could actually get him to read on his own or with me for a fifteen minute stretch at a time. Anyone who has had a child with reading difficulties can probably relate to my instant joy at this remarkable turn around. Better still was the fact that the enrichment program gave me a full report of what they had done, including his progress plotted on graphs from the beginning of the summer until the end. They had a closing conference with all parents and told us "we may find it beneficial to share the report with our child's school." I thought this was a wonderful benefit to the program since I could supply his new teacher with some background information on him from day one of the new school year. This could only benefit my son. The more a teacher knows about a student going in, the better for all concerned.

When he started second grade in the fall of that year, I arranged to meet with his teacher and his new Learning Disabilities tutor. I had also copied the report from summer to leave with both of them for reference. They both thanked me for the information and assured me that they would put it to good use in "getting to know his needs." That was reassuring to a mother who was new at dealing with a Learning Disability from this end. I felt confident that he was on the right path and he would have a good, successful school year. His teacher had also taught my older son second grade and I was quite impressed with her approach and kindness with children.

His second grade year went pretty smoothly. Everything was in place and he received some small group instruction in the mobile unit and some inclusion. I was pleased and started to relax about the whole thing by about November. As any parent of a child with needs knows, relaxing can be a dangerous thing. Pretty soon I began to notice things that didn't seem quite right to me. He began coming home with assignments with failing grades boldly written on the top of the paper. I should add that these assignments had to do with Reading, an area in which he had a Learning Disability. The first time it was a Health quiz. He had failed the test, not due to lack of knowledge about the material but because he was not able to accurately read the questions. This was readily apparent to me because I had quizzed him the night before this quiz and he had known all of the answers. I was extremely annoyed at first until I reminded myself that this "slip up" in communication between a Learning Disability teacher and regular education teachers often happens in schools. Logically, I knew this, but it was more annoying because it was my son this time. Technically when a child is on a Service Plan or an IEP in the area of Reading, a test or quiz in any other area (health, science, social studies) that involves reading should be read to the student or he/she should at least be given assistance in the reading portions. Otherwise, reading ability is really being tested and not the subject material. Once again, though, I'm sure the average parent would not know this.

When I called the school and spoke to his health teacher about this problem she was very understanding and accommodating. She was "totally unaware" that he had a Learning Disability in Reading and was more than willing to administer the test orally. Why she was "totally unaware" was frustrating and confusing to me but I was grateful for the outcome, namely that she understood and saw it as "no problem." The average school psychologist would have informed her of this, but it was becoming increasingly evident that this school was sadly lacking in that area. Many times in schools, teachers resist or resent this type of departure from their normal way of doing things. I was pleased to see the results a few days later. When he was tested orally on the material using different questions, he received 100%. This is proof of how parents must be informed and advocate for their children in these situations. Had I not intervened on his behalf, he would have received a failing grade on that and many other health tests/assignments to come. Once the teacher was aware, she went out of her way to accommodate his needs. So much in schools depends on good, reliable information and everyone in a child's day being informed of their needs. Someone had inadvertently dropped the ball in this case.

To prevent further incidents, I made a phone call to his Learning Disabilities tutor to ask that she please make sure all of his teachers knew he had been identified with a Learning Disability and what that meant in his day to day instruction. She assured me that she would take care of it and we had very few incidents the rest of the school year. If I had been a less informed mom or a more timid one, my son would have inevitably suffered and not performed up to his potential. I have found that approaching school personnel in an informed yet considerate manner where your children are concerned is always a wise choice. Most people involved in education respect this, and the results are usually favorable and everyone is happy. As a professional, I also respond better to people who come to me on behalf of their children with this attitude. Rudeness, anger and intimidation get you nowhere in schools or in life. I believe in the golden rule and try to live it. When you treat other people the way you would like to be treated you can never go wrong.

By the end of second grade he was steadily improving in reading and actually tolerating sitting with a book for pleasure for short periods of time. I use the word "tolerating" because I still had my doubts that he would ever enjoy reading, but at least he wasn't running anymore at the mere suggestion of the activity. He had definitely made gains and I was happy with the Learning Disabilities program at the school he attended. I had a good rapport with his LD tutor and felt like she advocated for my son in the regular education setting as much as she could. Being on the other side of the equation often and knowing first-hand how difficult it can be to get through to regular education teachers about students with special needs gave me a greater sense of appreciation. I was confident he was in the right place and he would only improve in the coming years.

Third grade brought more inclusion and less small group tutoring for him. He had received mostly small group instruction in the mobile unit in second grade with some inclusion. His LD tutor explained to me in the beginning of the year that she would be working closely with his third grade teacher and doing more inclusion since there were several students in his class with similar needs. Apparently, she would be present in the classroom several times a day, during reading and other academic subjects. She basically would circulate through the room and give individualized attention to students who were on a Service Plan. This was the growing trend in education at the time, but I remained somewhat skeptical about my son's individual needs being addressed appropriately. While I have always agreed that it is beneficial for students with identified needs to be treated like "regular" students as much as possible, I felt that his particular deficits in reading still required a great deal of individualized instruction in a one/one or one/small group setting. I wasn't sure this arrangement was ideal for my son or other students who were far below grade level in reading. Yes, the jury was still out on this new method in education. I was deliberating, and would wait patiently for all the evidence to be presented.

As I began to get to know my son's third grade teacher, I liked her more and more. She seemed to have a genuine concern for children and their overall well-being, which is always a good quality in a teacher. One example of this was her policy on making up work when a child was absent from school. My children are very healthy and rarely miss school. This despite the fact that they were not breastfed when they were infants and many assured me they would have every communicable disease due to my inexcusable maternal selfishness. I've never been an obsessive-compulsive clean freak either. Still, all of them have received "perfect attendance" awards many times. On the rare occasion when my older children had missed school however, they generally had massive amounts of homework sent home when they were sick. The logic of this has always confused me as a mother and an educator. First, I'm not sure making up "busy work" is ever beneficial to a student. I can see making up work that builds on some future concept like in math. Making up worksheets or seemingly mundane assignments when you are just getting over a fever, cold or stomach ailment seems ludicrous. What a way to insure a relapse and miss more school! I'm not sure why those assignments can't just be waived in the name of restoring good health and vitality. Second, if a given teacher is convinced they must be made up so everything is "fair" to the other students, doesn't it seem logical to give the student a week at least to complete the work? The only exception to this might be at the end of a quarter when the grades are due. I have often wondered why it is necessary to prop up a sick child in bed at home to complete assignments they missed at school because they were not well enough to attend. This can only result in one of two outcomes. The child becomes even sicker from stress, worry or sheer fatigue or the parents feel inclined to complete the assignments for their sick child, using juvenile writing and erasures that rip holes in the paper so no one will suspect their futile attempt at rescuing their child.

His third grade teacher, however, had a fresh, child-centered philosophy when a student was absent. I first became aware of this innovative policy when he missed two days early in the school year because of a bout with the flu. I had asked my older son to stop at his brother's classroom and ask the teacher for his homework. My oldest son, who was in sixth grade at the time came on and said, "She said his only homework is to feel better." Wow! Did I hear that right? What a concept. "Just feel better." My faith in humanity was restored. A teacher who not only claimed to care about kids but put a little muscle behind her words was rare in this setting. Yes, she quickly became one of my favorites. The added benefit for this teacher was that her students, my son included, were willing to work harder for her when they were well, because of the consideration she showed them when they were not up to par. The old Golden Rule at work again. Or maybe I should dub this the Circle of Respect. Either way, this refreshing attitude towards illness was embraced by parents and appreciated by students. I daresay more teachers and schools could benefit from this approach to absence.

His academic skills began to grow stronger in third grade. He was reading better every day and really enjoying school. Of course he had always enjoyed school. He had friends and never complained about attending. Because his needs in reading were identified at an early age (seven years) he kept a positive, happy outlook. I have known children who have struggled for years in school, received little if any assistance and have the appearance of being defeated and worn out at the tender age of ten or eleven. That is sad and often avoidable. I hesitate to assign blame for this because generally speaking many factors come into play in this scenario. Often teachers are ill informed about resource people in a school who could determine a child's needs, such as a school psychologist. In some schools, these resource people are not utilized in the most efficient manner or are not present at the school enough to be trusted by school personnel. Secondly, parents may be ill-informed, frustrated or not taken seriously by school personnel when they seek out help for their student. Some parents who lack education themselves may feel intimidated by school personnel and back down when faced with a student who is not achieving or displays behavior problems. Consequently, these students may "fall through the cracks" and merely get passed from grade to grade barely getting by academically and suffering from lack of motivation, low self-esteem and often increasingly negative feelings towards school and teachers in general. I felt fortunate that, because I knew my son was exhibiting signs of a Learning Disability at a young age and had that problem addressed, my son kept a positive attitude towards school. Many children are not this fortunate. By the end of third grade, I was quite pleased with his progress and so were his regular education teacher and Learning Disabilities Tutor. He would be due for a three year re-evaluation at the end of fourth grade and, if he continued to make such steady gains, it was possible he would no longer need special education services.

Chapter 8

The Middle Years

Fourth grade at the school my children attended was known to be difficult. I know for a fact, having worked in many schools over the years, that fourth grade at any school can be a real transition. This is typically when many schools stop "spoon feeding" students and expect much more individual initiative and follow-through on assignments. Still, I believed from my experience with my older two children that this particular school was way over the top with expectations for nine and ten year olds. Three and four hours of homework nightly seemed like a little much and was disproportionately high compared with the homework load of other grades at the school as well. I had sat at many meetings over the years where this topic was discussed and the basic answer from other parents and the administration was, "Well, once they get through fourth grade, the rest of the grades seem like nothing." Personally, I thought that was a lousy response to what seemed to be a growing problem at this Christian school but, as usual, I was the only one informed enough or naïve enough to think I could make a difference. People would agree with me in the parking lot or on the bleachers at a sporting event, but then they would conveniently forget every time the topic came up in the presence of the administration. "It does no good to speak up," was their way of justifying their apathy. Maybe so, but it never does much good to roll over and play dead either. The problem seemed to be "getting through fourth grade" with a good, healthy self-esteem and the love of school you had at the beginning of fourth grade. I knew many families who were not so lucky. Their children ended up despising school midway through fourth grade. It is difficult, if not impossible, to get back positive feelings towards school once they have been lost. As a school psychologist, I saw the damage these high demands were having on sensitive children, but no one seemed interested in changing anything. Thus, when my third child began fourth grade, I was skeptical to say the least. He had a different homeroom teacher than my other two children. At least there was hope that she would be more reasonable. She was new to the school that year, too, so I had no preconceived notions of her teaching methods and expectations.

I have always taken my children's lead where school issues are concerned. Although I did tell him "fourth grade might be tougher than third", I did not share my growing anxiety with him. Children with special needs in education have a difficult time meeting typical expectations but high expectations can be impossible if the teacher is not willing to accommodate their needs. The last thing children need is their parents worrying them unnecessarily about new experiences. I think as parents many times we do this unintentionally. We try to prepare our children and inadvertently plant seeds of doubt and anxiety that never would have been there had we not spoken. We manifest the exact thing we were trying to avoid. Of course every child is different, but he had always been apprehensive about new situations anyway, so I knew better than to delve into all my concerns about fourth grade. After all, he had seen his older sister and brother go through it, so he must have some idea of what was coming. In his case, I thought less information was better. I would merely watch from the sidelines and see what would develop. My son could quarterback the game and, if he needed me to, I'd run interference for him.

The beginning of the year went fine. He liked his new teacher, but there seemed to be some chaos and disruptions in the regular schedule due to the fact that his teacher was new. He would come home on many occasions and say, "We were supposed to change classes for math but no one told Mrs. Adams so we ended up being late." I'm sure this happens everywhere when someone is new to a work setting but there did seem to be a real lack of communication or lack of mentoring. I have seen mentoring to be very useful when a staff member is new to a school. Because every school and grade level routine is different, often a new teacher is paired up with a veteran teacher and can follow their example on a daily basis. This is more efficient and less chaotic for students and teacher alike. It also generally helps the new person feel more welcome and in control of new circumstances. Yes, after six years in this school setting my patience as an educator and a mom was beginning to wear thin.

Luckily, he didn't seem to have as much homework in fourth grade as my other two children, since his homeroom teacher was different. The two fourth grade classrooms did change classes, so he still had quite a bit of math homework. An hour and a half on one subject seemed excessive to me, but I had learned through experience that speaking up didn't accomplish much in this case, so I decided to keep my mouth shut this time. I listened to other parents complain about the excessive homework all year and waited patiently for someone to bring it up to the administration to no avail. Did I mention I am an optimist? Apathy is a problem in this country in general and in this fine educational institution it seemed to be an epidemic. The main thing to me was that he seemed to be tolerating fourth grade well with few complaints so I wasn't about to make waves. I had reached the inevitable conclusion all moms are faced with, it isn't always about me.

As fourth grade drew to a close, he was due to be re-evaluated for the Learning Disabilities program. According to state law, all children participating in Special Education must be re-evaluated every three years to insure that they are receiving the appropriate services. My son would be evaluated again at our local public school district since they were technically responsible for educating every child living in their district. I probably could have gone through the private school and had their psychologist do the evaluation, but since the public school did the initial evaluation, I thought this was the best way. I also did not have much confidence in the school psychologist at the private school and knew she was not present in the school much. When a child in a private school is evaluated by the public school district of residence, the Learning Disabilities Tutor and the regular education teacher at the private school typically give input regarding the student's strengths, weaknesses and behavior, and may even sit in on the evaluation meeting with parents. I was happy that the evaluation would be completed before the close of the school year so we could all plan for his needs in fifth grade well in advance.

When I called to schedule the re-evaluation with the public school district, I was happy to learn that their school psychologist was willing to travel to the private school where he was enrolled to do the evaluation. It was only a ten minute drive but some public schools want parents to bring the students to them, which is sometimes more chaotic, especially if you are a working parent (which I was). The school psychologist assured me that the evaluation would only take a few weeks which was a good thing. Although it was a different woman from the one who had first evaluated my second son, she sounded competent and pleasant on the phone, so I was happy.

The evaluation took about three weeks total and then I was called to the public school to discuss the results and recommendations. His special education teacher was also invited to the meeting, as well as a representative from the district where he was attending private school. That district would in effect be responsible for implementing the suggestions made, since we were choosing to have him attend a private school in a different district.

I knew he had made gains over the last three years but I was somewhat surprised by the magnitude of the gains. His reading had improved enough that he no longer had a significant gap between his ability and his reading achievement. He was reading about six months below grade level at this point. He had been reading over two years below grade level when he was first placed in the program, so that was impressive. Based on these results and his current daily achievement, the team assembled was recommending that he be dismissed from the Learning Disabilities Program for fifth grade and beyond. As a mother, I was thrilled, of course, but as a school psychologist, I had questions. Would he be monitored in the coming school year so that if he did have difficulty he could receive some additional help? Although the goal of any special education program is to dismiss students, withdrawing services totally sometimes has an adverse effect on students. I wanted to be sure that someone would be keeping an eye on his progress. I was satisfied when the Learning Disabilities Tutor said that she would monitor his progress and, if she needed to, she could step in on a remedial basis. That was music to an informed mother's ears.

He continued to do well in fifth grade and, except for some minor difficulties, I was pleased with his progress. He had always loved school but seemed to have a new found confidence since all of his "special" services were dropped. I have often seen this with children. The confidence parents and teachers put in them by in effect saying "you can do it on your own now" often propels them to new heights and even greater achievement. This is at least true with very motivated, intelligent children as my son was. Yes, he seemed to be on the right track. Choo-choo.

Chapter 9

Here We Go Again

When my second son was in fourth grade and my two oldest were in seventh and eighth grade, my youngest son, started preschool. The baby in the family had already completed three year old preschool at our local Community Church, but I thought he should be with his brothers and sisters for four year old preschool so I enrolled him at the private school. I'll admit this made life easier for mom, too. Having all the chicks in one place is always nice for the mother hen. In retrospect, maybe he should have stayed where he was. The Community Church had a four year old program also and the majority of the students were staying for that. I didn't know this at the time, but my last seemed to have difficulty adjusting to changes in routine and this decision probably did not help. He would also have difficulty making friends in the coming years and I would question whether this contributed to that.

He liked preschool at the new school and was thrilled that he would be able to see his brothers and sister in the hallways occasionally. He also had the same teacher and assistant that his brother had had earlier for preschool and he liked that idea. The two shared a room and his brother was always telling him about what he did in preschool and the younger one loved that connection. I had stayed home a few years when I had the last child but decided to go back to work, since the preschool had an extended care program where my youngest could stay after morning preschool. That way I would be able to work and could pick up all the kids at the same time. I had been itching to get back into a school for years and this seemed like the perfect chance. I had been home five years with him since he needed my attention and I never made enough to justify full time day care anyway.

About midway through preschool I was scheduled to have a conference with the preschool teacher. Apparently she was having conferences with all of the parents just to check progress. I remember asking if I could bring my son to the conference since I didn't have anyone to watch him. He accompanied me to his classroom and played around with all of the toys while his teacher and assistant and I talked about his progress. Normally I don't think it is appropriate for children to be present when adults talk about them but in this case I really did not have a choice. I had tried to get several friends to watch him and all were busy that day. I also think in preschool most children have little interest in what adults are saying if they are occupied with toys anyway.

His teacher showed me an assessment she had given which measured different areas of achievement in preschool and readiness for kindergarten. Apparently he had "not done well" on several of the sections. She had asked him "Where do you hang your coat?" He had responded "in the back hall." According to her this was incorrect because she was looking for "in the closet." As I told her, in our family we do have hooks in the back hall where he hangs his coat. Technically, he was correct, although that was not one of the acceptable responses printed. I am not faulting this teacher, with whom I had good rapport. The fact is she didn't seem interested in any alternative explanation. His answer was wrong according to her manual. Many times this happens in educational assessments and I have undoubtedly been guilty of marking things wrong that probably were very accurate for a given child. I do think some things have to be looked at on an individual basis. This was typical of many of my son's responses. He was not given credit because he had a different way of thinking than the average five year old. Not wrong – just different. Children are not black and white like printed responses. Unfortunately, many standardized assessments do not make allowances for this and teachers are baffled by what to do. The only one who suffers in this scenario is the child, who may look like he/she is clueless when in fact they are operating on a different, often more perceptive, level of thought. This was just the beginning of the complexities of my son. I have come to realize that many times he operates on a different plane than his peers. Many teachers since have seen this as a positive, intuitive side to my son. As an educator and a mother I have learned to appreciate this uniqueness. He has never been "typical" for his age.

The conclusion of this anxiety-provoking conference was that his preschool teacher thought "he should spend another year in preschool" to master some of the skills he lacked. He also was "very slow at completing tasks." What had she done about this? The jury was out on that. I actually considered her well-intentioned advice for a few days. Maybe he should? Maybe my perspective was all wrong? Maybe I was too close to the situation to be objective? After all, this was a woman who I respected and she had been wonderful with my older son previously. All of these thoughts go through a mother's head when you have been blindsided for the second time in a few years. Blindsided is never a good feeling. It is the feeling of being robbed of any of the crucial preparation time that goes into a monumental decision like retention. Yes, it is a monumental decision for most parents. I have since discovered at some schools it is not as monumental a decision, at least from the teacher's view. I would have liked to be forewarned of what was coming in this conference. I questioned her approach for days. Why hadn't she mentioned anything all year when I saw her every day before school? Surely some slight warning of the inevitable was indicated. No, idle chit-chat had been all she had offered up to that point of being hit in the head with a frying pan. Yes, that's what it felt like. On top of that, the other side of my head was still dented from the first fiasco a few years back. Was there no forethought to retention issues at this school? Didn't anyone offer guidance on how to approach parents about this topic? It baffled me from an educational standpoint and it insulted my intelligence as a parent of four children in this school. Anyone sitting on the receiving end of this conversation deserves more warning and consideration. What about a team decision? Where was the "team" that exists in most schools to discuss these life-altering recommendations? Where was the school psychologist? If nothing else, the mere fact that I knew something about this topic should have suggested bringing the principal in on the conversation. In my experience in schools, administrators are usually present for support for the teacher if nothing else. The whole thing was frustrating, annoying and totally inappropriate from an educational standpoint.

In fairness, the fact that my son "was very slow at completing tasks" was no surprise to me. He was very slow and inattentive at home also. I had been working to try and get him interested in writing and coloring for years. He didn't seem even mildly interested in either one. I bought him a coloring book every time he was remotely interested in the picture on the front. He loved trucks, trains and building and was hands-on with everything except pencils and crayons. The coloring books sat unused except for the ten minute intervals when I could coax him into sitting beside me and "using all the wonderful colors." To be honest, I'm sure there was usually some bribery involved. His lack of fine motor skills and pencil grip had concerned me for a while. He wasn't picking up on shoe tying either. Every time he had a birthday (three, four and five years old), I decided "he has to learn to tie his shoes" and every time, I ended up defeated, after he struggled and struggled with no success. Of course, as any mother knows, it is one thing to notice things about your child, it is quite another to have someone else point them out and label them as "problems." Again, I'm sure I had unwittingly done this to parents throughout my career. It doesn't feel as good when you are on the receiving end of "problems" that might affect school.

After stewing about this for a few days and considering all the pertinent facts, I decided I was not in favor of retention for my youngest son. For many of the same reasons I had declined with his brother, I felt it would do more harm than good. An additional deciding factor was that my youngest has a January birthday. As such, he has always been right in the middle of his class by age. Retention is successful mainly with young boys. He was not young. If he had difficulties, they would likely continue with or without retention. I knew I had to stick to my informed decision about this. I knew it was in his best interests to move on to kindergarten with his peers.

Likewise, I knew it would be an unpopular decision at this school. It seemed to me like no one questioned much of anything that was recommended at this supposedly excellent school. Did I mention my disdain for apathy? Right or wrong, no one was going to quiet my voice about this. Only time would tell if I had made the right decision. Either way it was my decision alone. And alone I felt, believe it. No team, no support for my opinion or the teachers. I think a team would have served us both well and I was baffled and disappointed – again. The team concept that was alive and well most places was missing here.

I requested another meeting with his teacher a few weeks later. I informed her that I wanted him screened for kindergarten. Barring any earth shattering results of those, I would be sending him on. Kindergarten screening is usually done late in the school year and assesses readiness for kindergarten in five year olds. It was designed to prevent school failure by identifying areas where students need additional help over the summer to prepare for success in kindergarten. Rarely is it recommended that a child not attend kindergarten based on these results. She assured me that he would be screened if that is what I wanted, but she did have her reservations.

I think it was at this point that I began to seriously considering switching my youngest to a public school for kindergarten. As much as I knew from an educational standpoint, this warranted consideration from a mother's standpoint – the mere though tore at my gut. I had attended private schools for sixteen years (including college) and supported them in every way. I had worked in them for ten years at that point. Private schools were in my blood. I believed in them and had always pictured all of my children attending them. I vowed to relax and put off any decisions until I had the results from the kindergarten screening. I had the added advantage of knowing exactly what was on the kindergarten screening, since I administered it at my school, and was confident he would do fine. Yes, if they were planning on using those results to keep him out of kindergarten they were out of luck. No, I wasn't planning on administering the whole battery to him before the scheduled date. Although I'd be lying if I said the thought never crossed my mind, I do have scruples! I also sincerely wanted a fair estimate of my son's readiness for kindergarten. I may be a mother first but I also had learned to appreciate this process as a school psychologist and respected it as a good one. I would not sacrifice the integrity of my profession or my son's best interests for my own gains.

Of course kindergarten screening day was a nerve racking one for me. My son was fine and took it all in stride. I prepared him in all the ways I knew were appropriate. I gave him the usual speech I had learned so well and given to children many times before they began the screening. "You will work with many different ladies at different tables. It will all be fun, so just try your best." And of course, "It is important that you do your best and finish everything." I also had him go to the bathroom (twice) before we left the house so he wouldn't have to interrupt the process. He seemed to progress though it fine as I waited in the hallway outside of the school gym with the other moms. This was definitely not the time to share information about my profession. Many moms had questions about the procedures and I filled them in as best I could without revealing how I knew. Somehow I suspected some might suspect my son had an advantage which he did not. I know how these competitive moms of the twentieth century are. We all wanted out child to do their best and make us look wonderful in the process. Most of us wished we could be a fly on that wall. One mother actually had the nerve to ask me:

"I wonder if we can see how they are doing through the window on the gym door?"

"No" I responded without hesitation. "I already tried ten minutes ago, they covered them up."

Did I mention motherhood takes precedence over my other profession? I am just as nervous in these situations as the uninformed parent. As the school psychologist, I would have covered them too. It was the thing to do, but I did not appreciate being on the other side of the construction paper that was obstructing my view of my son's progress.

When he came out after about an hour I asked him how it went.

"Oh, pretty good. Some lady told us all the stuff you told me in the beginning and I told her I already knew it all. Then she asked us to go to the bathroom and I told her I did – twice."

Yeah, thanks for sharing. I'm sure my parent rating was going up by the minute.

"What did you like the best?" I inquired on the way to the car.

"The best part was when I played under the table."

Great, I could see the notes scrawled in the margin of whatever test booklet that was now. "Student is immature, distractible, poor listening skills, difficulty following directions." I had written them all about some other person's child. Funny, they seemed like just "behavioral observations" at the time. Now they seemed like branding on my son's forehead.

I was scheduled to meet with the veteran kindergarten teacher two weeks later to discuss the results of the screening. I was actually pretty calm about the whole thing. Despite the "under the table" issue, I was confident he had done reasonably well. By reasonably well I meant he would not be in the group of students who perform "below expectancy" in over half of the areas and are thus recommended to "wait a year" for kindergarten. As I recall, my prediction was close to right. He scored above expectancy in several areas, at expectancy in three, and below expectancy in two. She did mention that he was off task a great deal and directions had to be repeated often. All things I had heard before (and would hear again). She basically said the decision was mine whether he went to kindergarten or stayed in preschool for another year. "No one has a crystal ball... ya, da... ya, da, ya, da." If I had a dime for every time I had said those comforting/frustrating words. I left there assured that the results were fine from where I stood and my youngest was going to kindergarten. Nothing in that profile convinced me otherwise. He might be distractible and have difficulty following directions for years whether he spent another year in preschool or not. It seemed like no one had shown me why he should do that. It was the same curriculum, same teacher. No game plan or interventions mentioned. What would be different? The only answer I came up with was my son's love for school and happy personality. That might be different. If he was distractible now, another year of the same thing might make it worse, not better. He was bright, I knew that. The school didn't know it. No mention was made of finding out through an evaluation either. This situation was really getting under my skin.

When I shared my decision with his preschool teacher she suggested,

"If you need him to go to kindergarten we want you to stay at this school."

I'm sure I may have used this terminology over the years too. The "needs" of parents often do outweigh what is in the best interest of their children. I get that. All day kindergarten is a godsend for working mothers. Nevertheless, I felt insulted by this remark. I wasn't some run of the mill parent whose needs were overshadowing what was in my son's best interests. I was informed, and had given up endless hours of sleep over this. It wasn't a decision I was making casually. This teacher's off the cuff remark about my needs seemed careless at best but I'm sure she did not intend it that way. Once again, sitting on the other side of this conversation made me ponder every remark I had ever made to parents about retention. The topic sure seems different when you are in the hot seat. God knew what he was doing putting me there. As painful as this was, I was to realize only years later it served a purpose in making me a more compassionate resource for parents who walk this same road. I would never again presume to know the "needs" of another parent. Actually I never assume anything anymore. It is ignorant, inconsiderate and selfish to think that everyone thinks like you do.

I assured her that I would undoubtedly keep him in the school. I also took the opportunity to inquire,

"Do you think your school psychologist could observe him and see what she thinks?"

"Oh, I doubt it, we've asked her to do things before and she does nothing. She's only here one day."

Well, isn't that a great testimony to my profession! I realize that sometimes teachers don't know what a school psychologist actually does, but most know they can call on a school psychologist to at least observe and give their opinion. I like to think I have always been a valuable resource for teachers and administrators at the schools where I was assigned so this perception bothered me, to say the least. The perception that she could not count on the school psychologist to do anything was troubling. The most frustrating part, however, was that she was employed by the same company that I was. Ever hear the expression, "caught between a rock and a hard place?" What could I do? Nothing – if I wanted to keep my job. Easy answer but frustrating doesn't even begin to cover it. I knew what a valuable resource a school psychologist could be for my son and there wasn't one available to me. Yes, the prospect of him staying at this school was beginning to look dismal at best. But I resolved to try kindergarten and see where that led. I did ask his preschool teacher for a recommendation on which of the two kindergarten teachers would be best for the needs of my son. She said she would think about it and get back to me.

I am an activist. I actively try to change things I feel are wrong. I crave justice. I speak up when I need to. I take a stand when one needs to be taken. No one in my high school class would ever believe this about me. I was the "quiet" one in school and was endlessly teased about it. The term wasn't around then but I do believe I was bullied for years because I dared to be quiet. I was the one who followed the crowd and worked at being seen and not heard. Somewhere in adulthood, this all changed and I began finding my voice and using it when I felt the need. Maybe it was all the years of pent up vocalization that pushed me over to the other side. I firmly believe I am assertive and not aggressive when I need to be. I voice my opinions in a nice way, but when I believe in a cause, I refuse to quiet my voice. I've often wondered if God was saving my voice for the important causes he wanted me to crusade for later. This crusade was testing me.

Over the next few weeks, months and years actually, this whole lack of school psychology services at this school festered in my gut like rotten food trying to work through the digestive system. I tried to expel it in the usual ways I deal with stress. I ran more, I read good uplifting books, and I prayed. I asked God to show me what to do. I wracked my brain thinking how I could somehow take a stand on this and make a difference. I like to make a difference and often I feel compelled to. If not me, who? This was a compulsion like one I had never felt. I truly felt God was telling me to do something. I was in a unique position to do it. But what could I do? It felt like my hands were tied. My mouth was bound in duct tape. Yes, I was a prisoner of my employer at this point. I contemplated many things. I tried to "let it go" as friends and family advised. Letting it go is wise in theory. In practice it is difficult when your profession and advocating for children is embedded in your soul. In the end I resolved that if I was meant to right this wrong God would show me the way. Faith was essential and patience was necessary if my son was to continue in kindergarten at this school. One day at a time became my new philosophy.

I had a conversation with his preschool teacher a few weeks later. She had decided which kindergarten teacher she thought would be best for his needs. I must say, although I was open to the suggestion, I wasn't totally in agreement right off the bat. My next oldest son, who was the only one of my children to have attended kindergarten at this school, had the other teacher. I had good rapport with this woman and was familiar with her teaching style. I thought she was a wonderful, compassionate woman. I felt comfortable with her. Why start with someone new? Like most of my species, I function better in my comfortable, familiar world. I don't much like stepping out of my comfort zone. As she explained her reasoning, however, I began to see the light and thought this might be the wiser choice given the circumstances. I was unfamiliar with the teacher she was recommending but supposedly she was "less structured." Yes, that could be good for my youngest. She was "more adaptable when students had needs." That sounded good too. Yes, maybe this would be best. "Alright" I heard myself saying, "I guess we'll go with her." She went on to say that she would voice this opinion when the teachers talked about class placements at the end of the year. Great, I was all ready for summer and swimming in a cold neighborhood pool. I was ready to soak my head and forget my academic worries. Ready to let my youngest just be what he was for a few months without agonizing over every detail of his development and questioning everything I had done with him since birth. Who was I kidding? There was still the inevitable shoe-tying to be accomplished. Here we go again. Let the good times roll!

Chapter 10

Twinkle, Twinkle Little Star

When I was in kindergarten, we played with blocks, we went to see a farm and we sang. I remember *Twinkle, Twinkle Little Star* was my favorite. I loved it. It was magical and I could actually see the stars shinning in the sky when I sang it. I took me away to places only a five year old can go. I loved kindergarten. Mrs. Millman was my first formal teacher. I thought her name was Mrs. Milkman. After all, she did take us to a farm where we learned to milk a cow and churn butter. It seemed like a natural progression. After all – she was Mrs. Milkman. I never realized that her real name was Millman until my mother corrected me many years later when I was retelling a story from that time. I don't remember letters and numbers being a part of kindergarten. If they were they were a small part. I certainly don't have much memory of that. I know my mother and other mothers at the time never worked with us at home before kindergarten. Few of us went to preschool back then and, if we did, they were usually co-ops run by moms.

Anyone who has children knows that kindergarten is much different now. It has changed significantly even in the twenty years I have been involved in education. Some young parents do not realize this. They are convinced their children can enter kindergarten and learn their letters and numbers there. Wrong. Although most preschools work on letters and numbers, children fare better if they are at least exposed to them by two or three years of age. Many yuppies actually teach their children to read before they enter kindergarten. The pros and cons of this can be argued, but the fact is that schools have advanced a great deal since the 60's and 70's. There may still be music, but it is a small part of the day. "Twinkle, Twinkle" has probably been replaced by some state standard that needs to be accomplished for schools to receive funds. I'm not knocking that. I understand state standards. I am, in fact, a part of the system that uses them and relies on them to judge the progress of students. Still, sometimes I long for more simple times when a five-year old could sing "Twinkle, Twinkle" and count on mom to tie her shoes. When students had time to choose five different colors and leisurely finish a masterpiece instead of rushing through the process to get on to the next pertinent task to be accomplished in the school day. When competition was limited to building wood structures, not reading by the time you are four years old so you might compete for a "gifted" program.

In my experience, the majority of children come to school with readiness skills. Their parents have gotten the word. Teach them letters and numbers, read to them, show them how to use a pencil and write their name. And the command of all commands, not too much television or they will never amount to any good. I could debate the pros and cons of television watching until the cows come home I suppose. Suffice it to say that I am confident that my children learned a great deal from shows like Sesame Street and Mr. Rogers in their younger years. As my children grew older they also profited greatly from the History Channel and The Learning Channel. Granted some things I would rather they not learn, but isn't that where parenting skills come into play? Thinking that television is all bad is simplistic at best.

With so many women working outside of the home, more and more children enter preschool and kindergarten with several years of some type of academic instruction under their belts. This is probably more the norm these days. There have been times in my educational career, however, when I have been surprised to see that there are still some children who do not attend preschool in any form before being enrolled in kindergarten. These children typically fall into two categories. There are those whose mothers really work with them at home from an early age and provide an enriching, stimulating home environment. These children typically have socialization worked into their daily schedule as well, either with younger siblings or with neighbors, friends where "play dates" are arranged. In this case, the home can be as adequate, if not better, than any formal preschool setting. These are typically mothers who have been teachers themselves and decided to stay home with their young children or mothers who are well educated and value education. I have found this category of children to be rare, however. This is undoubtedly due to the growing trend of women working outside of the home and not being available to provide this. The second group of children who do not attend preschool is the more common, although still relatively rare. These children typically are in homes where the parents are either young or first time parents and clearly do not realize how advanced the kindergarten curriculum has become in the last thirty years. They assume that kindergarten is or "should be" as it was "when I was five." I have had parents actually tell me, "Well, it shouldn't be that way" when I have tried to explain why their kindergartner is behind in October or November. Unfortunately people who design curricula rarely take a poll of parents' desires. Even if they did, I'm sure most parents, in our fast-paced world, would want things just the way they are. Since most of us are always trying to keep with the Jones', of course we want our kids to keep up with the Jones' kids too.

At a school where I worked for many years, although we routinely did kindergarten screening in March, there were typically one or two children who started out the kindergarten year clearly unprepared. Somehow these students managed to do adequately on the kindergarten screening but had difficulties right off the bat with the day-to-day demands. I remember one little boy in particular who had little concept of letters and numbers, could not write his name, had limited socialization skills and also had weak language skills. In this boy's case, it turned out he had enrolled late in the summer and thus did not go through the kindergarten screening at all. Needless to say, he came up on his teacher's radar within the first week of the new school year. By the first month of school, she was burned out and was desperately seeking help from the school psychologist, who happened to be me. She had several meetings that first quarter with the parents and was desperate for some answers about how to work with this student, who stood out as being so far behind the rest of the class. The teacher informed me that the boy was the only student in her class who had not attended preschool. As I recall, he was also young for the class.

At the initial meeting I had with the parents and teacher, it became apparent that these parents were very uninformed about kindergarten in 2007. They had assumed he would "learn numbers and letters at school." They really didn't even seem very concerned about his obvious difficulties with speech and language skills. "That's just the way he is," seemed to be their justification for everything. It became readily apparent that, although the mother did not think it was necessary for the boy to attend preschool, she had done little in the way of readiness skills at home. Also, his lack of having experience in a formal classroom setting was readily becoming apparent to the teacher and his classmates. Simple classroom behaviors such as sitting still, raising your hand before speaking and waiting for your turn in activities were beyond to this student. Although the teacher initially labeled these behaviors as "distractible" and "inattentive" to me when we spoke, I pointed out that it was possible that he just had not learned these things in a preschool setting as other children had. He was also an only child and seemed to have limited exposure to other children, so he probably had not learned these classroom skills at home either. In my opinion, there is a fine distinction between never having learned a skill and having a deficit in that area. It seemed obvious that he had never learned to raise his hand, sit still or wait his turn – things most children learn in preschool or before. I think the same can be said of Attention Deficit Disorder (ADD). Although I firmly believe many students are correctly labeled with this disorder and it affects every area of school learning, it is a diagnosis that warrants scrupulous consideration. On observing the parenting skills of some parents and their family routines, it becomes obvious that some families do not promote or encourage attending and listening skills. If these skills are not taught, reinforced and valued at a young age, a child cannot be expected to magically embrace them upon entering a classroom. Never having learned to attend is not Attention Deficit

Disorder. Attention Deficit Disorder is being inattentive and distracted even when structure and situations to foster attention have been in place from an early age. I believe it is a true diagnosis for some children, my son included. I also believe it is overused and sometimes invalid.

In the case of this little boy I saw at my school, it seemed like maybe he just hadn't learned some of the skills associated with kindergarten success. In late September or early October I met with the teacher, the principal and the boy's parents to discuss what we believed would be a viable solution to all of his difficulties. The teacher and I had met with the principal previously and laid all our cards on the table, so to speak. Because his skills overall were lacking and he was functioning more like a preschooler, we suggested that they consider withdrawing the boy and enrolling him in a preschool. The ultimate goal was to prepare him to re-enroll in the school the following year, better prepared to succeed in kindergarten. This may not have been suggested if we had a preschool at this school, but we did not. He could go to preschool without any of the social embarrassment that might have been felt in the same school. This is not a common suggestion, however, and not one any of us took lightly. In my twenty years as a school psychologist, I have never recommended this before. It was very unique to this situation and this boy's needs. I truly felt like if we kept him in kindergarten we were basically robbing him of the preschool experience which he needed in order to adequately prepare for kindergarten, and we were also taking the parents' tuition money under false pretenses. The kindergarten teacher would not be able to give him the attention he needed or scale down the curriculum to meet his needs. It seemed like the best solution for everyone concerned.

When we met with the parents and went over their son's progress in the first month of school, it was obvious they still didn't understand how behind he was. They kept talking about how he would "catch up." The point we tried to get across is that we were not at all convinced he would "catch up", and he would also just get more and more frustrated by trying to. The idea of putting him in preschool seemed interesting to the mother, but the father was dead set against it.

This was a familiar scenario to me, as I had seen it many times in my career. If anyone was going to resist a change in placement for a student, it was typically the father. I find this usually happens for two reasons. One, fathers typically spend less time with children, which means they know their needs less and they also are less frustrated by trying to help and finding out you have run out of ideas. Secondly, anything "different" about sons especially seems to be a blow to the male ego. Many men take it personally that something may be "wrong" with their sons. I don't want to overanalyze why this may be, but suffice it to say it is a pattern I have seen many times with boys who have academic or behavioral difficulties. To say it is frustrating to teachers and school psychologists, who typically are women, would be a gross understatement. Often it hampers the implementation of services that might well help a student succeed. On many occasions I have wanted to scream at a father, "Get over it already, your son needs some help here." Or maybe, "It isn't all about you." Of course my mouth would never utter these words for fear of losing my job, but a less rational psychologist might be equipped with a frying pan for these frustrating members of the male species. Yes, I have often longed to knock some sense into the male ego.

At the end of this conference the parents did say they would "seriously consider" placing their son back in preschool and get back to us soon. We did stress that a decision should be made in the next several weeks if he was to transition to preschool early in the school year. The principal and teacher even suggested a local preschool that happened to have an opening and were willing to take him. The principal offered to refund the tuition the family had previously paid. Yes, everything was in place for the change in placement, now came the waiting game. Would they consider all the information and data we had presented and agree that it was in their son's best interest to switch him to preschool? Only time would tell. I, for one, was hopeful. I really had a fondness for this boy and sincerely believed he would benefit from a year in preschool. He needed to experience the socialization, structure and academic readiness skills he had skipped. I had put a lot of time and research into really believing in this decision for this family. In the end though, of course, as the parents it was their decision. The old saying about "you can lead a horse to water but you can't make him drink" really applies here.

Two weeks later the teacher had yet to hear from the parents regarding their decision. The student was falling further and further behind and we were all getting concerned. After numerous attempts to reach the mother, she finally connected. The mom told the teacher that they had decided to keep him in kindergarten. "If he ends up having to repeat, we'll understand that." Also adding, "We'll work with him more at home." We were all disappointed by this decision, but I feel confident I have probably also disappointed some teachers with decisions I have made about my children. It's not about disappointing others, it's about making the best decision for your children with the information you have. These people clearly were doing what they thought best and who could fault them for that? We were left with the fact that we would have to do intensive interventions to get this child through kindergarten. I guess the goal was not to merely get him through, but to help him grow and maintain his enthusiasm for school. Often, when students struggle, enthusiasm and motivation are the first to go. Self-esteem follows and I did not want this boy to loose either one. He was a real smiley, happy little boy in spite of his difficulties and we wanted him to finish the kindergarten year with the same happy-go-lucky attitude. He did benefit from many successful interventions that were put into place with everyone involved. By the end of the year, however, he still was not prepared for first grade and so repeating kindergarten was recommended to the parents. They chose to take him to a different school and we really did not know until months later that they had taken our advice. Many parents who leave a school choose to enroll their child in the next grade even if they suspect that may not be the best choice. This may be a form of denial or showing the first school that the child can and will make it in the next grade. Who's to say? There is the chance they feel like a different school will make a difference. When we found out this boy was repeating kindergarten in November of the next school year, we were happy and hopeful he would make gains.

With all of this information rolling around in my head, I was a little apprehensive when my youngest son was entering kindergarten that fall. The stage had been set for me to wonder and worry whether he would be able to measure up. Of course I also had my own sons past difficulties running through my mind and had come to observe that their developmental milestones were similar in many ways. After all, the gene pool was alike and they did share the same bedroom. Nature and nurture can't get much closer than that. It had been drilled into my head for years that those two factors intermingle to predict achievement and overall success in life.

So with new tennis shoes that had laces and a new backpack full of supplies, my youngest headed off to kindergarten that fall of 2005. Although he hadn't mastered shoe tying, he was at least comfortable with the idea of attempting it every time he put on his shoes. Although he was looking forward to kindergarten, my youngest was still talking about missing his preschool teacher. To say that my son has a difficult time with moving on and changing would be an understatement. Most kids love birthdays, he didn't for the first seven years of his life. "I don't want to turn four" was what we would hear as the big day approached. "I want to stay three forever." Looking back, I think I made the mistake once of commenting that he was "getting bigger" and "growing up" when he was turning three or four. I think he took it to heart and was nervous, anxious or worried about the prospect. It is only now that he is nine that he finally likes birthdays. I think he finally believes that you can still play with trains even if you are older than five. Maybe he finally sees that all the fun isn't sucked out of life by the time you hit six or seven.

When I finally convinced him that his new teacher might be fun, too, he headed out the door ready to conquer the kindergarten world his brothers and sister had filled him in on. Of course he had to be reassured several times that it would be o.k. to say "hi" to his former teacher if he saw her in the hallway. Yes, change is difficult. Sometimes even for moms.

Part of me was excited and part of me was wondering what new skills beyond shoe tying would prove challenging this year. Being the eternal optimist, however, I decided that my son would inevitably follow my lead into this new and different world of kindergarten. I'd better walk in smiling and full of the enthusiasm my son needed from me in order to excel.

Within the first few days of kindergarten his new teacher sent home an informational sheet for each parent to complete on their child. This consisted of developmental milestones, likes and dislikes and strengths and weaknesses. Basically anything that would give her some background on the child and help her to become familiar with her students. Good idea in theory. Being the overly thorough type of mom that I am and realizing the importance of background information in education, I provided everything I could think of. I discussed at length his difficulty with fine motor skills including writing and shoe tying, stressing that we continued to practice these throughout the summer. I also stated that although I had difficulty understanding him and thought he might qualify for speech services he had been screened in preschool by the speech and language pathologist at the school and he did not qualify. She thought it was a developmental problem and eventually he would learn the sounds he lacked.

It was with utter surprise then when I received a note in the first week saying that my son had to learn to "tie his shoes as soon as possible." I was taken aback to say the least. Actually to be honest I was insulted, baffled and down right angry. First of all, I clearly had stated on my form that he had "fine-motor delays." I had also stated that we were "working on shoe-tying with limited success." Had she read the forms? If so, was that note really necessary after one week of school?

She also was well aware that he had been recommended for retention and I had declined. Doesn't that warrant some extra patience with a mom who is probably nervous about the whole kindergarten process? Where was the compassion and understanding? The other factor involved the preschool curriculum. To my knowledge they had never worked on shoe tying the year before. If she expected every child to enter kindergarten tying shoes shouldn't that be covered in the preschool curriculum? At the very least, parents should be told to work on it over the summer. Did it have to be such an issue? Still, as always, I resolved to calm myself and look at it from the teacher's perspective. She did have twenty four students, and if each one needed their shoes tied, it could present a problem and take away from instruction. It was just possible I was overreacting. Possible I said – not probable. After all, I am the calm reasonable type.

The next day I had put the note out of my mind when I went to pick up my son after school. Waiting in the parking lot with the other kindergarten moms, I started chatting with the grandmother of a boy in my son's class. I had never met the woman before but after we began making idle conversation she introduced herself as "John's grandmother." Midway through the conversation she inquires,

"Can your son tie his shoes yet?"

"Funny you should ask", I said, trying to keep the steam from escaping my ears.

"My son and daughter-in-law got a note from the teacher yesterday that seemed a little over the top."

Grandma obviously had the gift of tact in conversation. She went on to say that several other parents had also gotten the note. All boys, I might add. The expression "misery loves

104

company" came to mind. At least my son wasn't the only one being singled out and it's always good to have your opinion validated. From an educational standpoint, I was just shocked that this teacher wasn't more aware of developmental lags with young boys. Although some five year olds can tie their shoes, there are many who do not master this task until they are six or seven years old. I might be able to understand sending a note like this home mid-way through kindergarten, but the first week seemed inappropriate, unnecessary and lacked forethought.

Being the politically correct person I am I responded with a note that basically said, "We'll continue to work on it." Of course part of me wanted to suggest that if it was so important maybe the kindergarten aid could take a small group of kids and work on it at school daily. I'm sure there was some time during the day when they could sneak that in to the curriculum if it was so crucial to succeeding in kindergarten. Did I mention that I am the helpful type? I just wasn't sure the teacher would see it as being "helpful" so I decided to refrain – this time. Over the years I've come to realize there is a fine line between being "helpful" and "controlling" and I wanted to keep the peace with this teacher at this point in the school year. We had a long way to go.

Another time early in the school year, his teacher phoned me to discuss an incident that happened before school. Seems he had somehow wandered down the hallway before school hours. I had thought he was being supervised in the area designated as extended care. She had phoned to try to sort out exactly what had happened in this incident. Some time during the course of the conversation she mentioned that she'd been meaning to phone me anyway to discuss his awkward pencil grip. "He holds his pencil like a two-year old" was her exact comment. Well, that stings, to say the least. I was about at the boiling point by now but calmly replied, "Yes, he has fine motor delays as I noted on the form you sent home. We work on it daily."

Why was I beginning to feel like my son had been black-balled since day one in kindergarten? Was I overreacting? Quite possibly, but all of this drama in the first few weeks of school was not helping the overanxious mother in me. The school psychologist in me knew that I had been forthcoming about all of his issues and what we were doing about them. The professional still strongly believed none of these things were major factors in whether a boy would be successful in kindergarten if given the right support and encouragement. I think the key would be early interventions if he needed them and I think the jury was still out on that. I felt like a rush to judgment was occurring and I was not the least bit pleased. What was the teacher proposing to do about these delays in fine motor skills? Nothing had been mentioned about that. What was the plan from her end? In retrospect, this would probably have been a good time for me to ask to meet with the school's Intervention Assistance Team. I could have at least asked, I suppose but the fact that past experience had shown me that either they didn't have one or rarely used it, made the prospect of anything happening unlikely at best.

Many times in schools, teachers deal with vast numbers of students and parents in any given year. Sometimes the caring and compassion is lost in the curriculum goals. Often teachers do not really take the time to get to know the students and parents assigned to their classrooms before the school year begins. Had this teacher taken the time to read over the form she had sent home and familiarize herself with my son, perhaps the note about shoe tying and the phone conversation might have been unnecessary. What both of those things accomplished was to put me on the defensive and make me doubt this teacher's knowledge of developmental milestones with young boys. I'm not sure to this day if that response was appropriate but it was a gut reaction based on who I am and my educational background. Had the teacher taken the time to read over the form more carefully, she also would have known I was a school psychologist. It is important to know parents' educational backgrounds and expectations for their children. That might have been important information in her interactions with me. I'm not sure if the preschool teacher had a conversation with her about my background and the difficulties she perceived my son to have in preschool. Being proactive is typically stressed in education. Maybe we could have all met and discussed interventions before the school year began? In retrospect, I wish I had suggested that. Of course that is something a school psychologist usually suggests. I was a mother in this scenario and was desperately trying to stay in that role. It was getting more difficult by the day. Where was the school psychologist? It might have been helpful to have one involved in any case where retention was suggested but especially in this one. It was beginning to become apparent that she wasn't involved in any of the traditional roles of a school psychologist. Why wasn't someone seeking her out on behalf of my son? It was becoming increasingly clear that many of the teachers at this "excellent" educational establishment had no idea how a school psychologist might benefit them and their students. I didn't blame the teachers. After all, you can't miss what you've never had. The public relations part of school psychology that is so vital to the role was obviously missing. In order to have good communication in a school this size, it was necessary to be present more than a few hours a week and build rapport. Inadequate services seemed to have fostered apathy and disinterest in normal educational procedures. There was a definite breakdown in the system here and it was directly impacting students and families. If it was impacting my student and my family, it was probably impacting others too.

Somewhere near the middle of his kindergarten year, the teacher requested that mothers to come in once a month and a help with Centers in the classroom. Centers are commonly used in kindergarten to promote different skills like listening, language, visual discrimination and others necessary to be successful. Since I was working part-time and had a few days free, I volunteered to help. After all, helpful is my middle name. I also get along well with young children and have experience working with them, too. My secondary motive was being able to see my son from a different perspective and maybe observe what his teacher saw during the school day. But then again, can you ever really see a tiny person who you carried for nine months and love dearly in an objective light? I wasn't sure, but knew I had to try. I wasn't blind to the possibility of him acting differently when mom was around. Yes, I would put on my school psychologist hat and try to see him from that perspective. If a professional wasn't available to observe, I would have to do it myself. When a job needs to be done, I do it.

I learned a lot from that weekly interaction with my son and his classmates. He loved the idea that I was going to be in his classroom once in a while. That alone seemed positive.

The impact of a child knowing that their parent cares enough to make time to come to school and be involved can't be overstated. I know many people who constantly make excuses about why they are not involved in their children's school. People are busy, but prioritizing for your children is important and will reap huge benefits in their lives. Prioritizing works both ways. Be present but do not smother. There is a fine distinction. Don't let their activities or needs consume you. I learned that his teacher had many fine qualities I value in an educator. She was organized, loving, and she seemed to have a happy classroom. I tried to put aside my preconceived notions and see her objectively. I tried to do the same for my son. I tried to be fair. I pride myself on being fair.

It became clear from the beginning of my visits that my youngest was off task quite a bit of the time. He had to be refocused many times in simple activities. Still, he did eventually focus and do what was expected. He was not a behavior problem as far as acting out or disrupting other students. He basically disrupted himself. Another thing became readily apparent too. There were other students who were far more disruptive from an educational standpoint. Several of the boys I worked with were loud, out of their seats more than they were in them, and annoying to other students. My son had none of these behaviors. Were they on the teacher's radar? One had to wonder. The mother in me accepted his difficulties. They were real and I could see that first-hand. The school psychologist in me wanted to make a list of the others I was concerned about. I refrained though – sticking to my role. "I am the mother and not the school psychologist." Say that five times to yourself and believe it! But, it certainly can be difficult not to throw out the lifeboats when you see people drowning and there is no rescue team.

As the school year progressed, so did my son. Maybe he wasn't as on task as the other children and his reading was still lagging behind, but he was making progress for himself. That is all I could ask. I continued to get notes occasionally about unfinished work or inattentive behavior. Apparently he wasn't coloring fast enough and had to miss free time often to complete papers. He never liked coloring. Most boys don't. I guess I've never understood why this is a big deal to some primary teachers. I've never seen coloring on a resume or considered it an important life skill. I also noticed that he had an artistic, creative flare like his older sister. He preferred to take his time and color things differently and precisely, unlike some four and five-year-olds, who use the same two colors and basically scribble everything. Obviously creativity and artistic ability was not fostered in this school. Again, I don't blame the teacher. I blame the system and curriculum goals. She had deadlines to meet. But if I realized this about my son, couldn't she? He was clearly bright and was developing an extensive vocabulary. He had many good qualities. Like any mom, I longed to hear about those. To date, that seemed to be missing. Accentuate the positive – it is a basic premise of education and life! It can make all the difference in relationships.

In February, I was scheduled to conference with my son's teacher. I was feeling pretty good about the conference because it was scheduled after report cards were distributed and he had received S's (satisfactory) in everything and actually two O's (outstanding). I believe he did receive one N (needs improvement) in Reading. Of course it was also noted that he was distractible and inattentive. The teacher began the conference talking about how he had made progress and she was seeing "big changes" in his coloring and art work. She could "hardly believe it was the same boy." That is a direct quote. She was beginning to see his artistic ability and took me out in the hallway to see some of his drawings. I choked back tears. He was finally going to be o.k. in the eyes of this school. I had never doubted it but they had always acted like his problems were monumental. I never thought so but what do I know? After all I only have a Masters in Education and an Educational Specialist Degree. However, I am astute enough though never to bring this up at a school my children attend. I have learned to take my degrees with a grain of salt when my children are involved. I know realistically that my emotions have a tendency to get in the way of my intellectual base. In other words, my son had the potential of reducing me to Jell-O with his big brown eyes. Like any mother lion, I will protect my cub at all costs.

Towards the end of the conference that was going well from my perspective his teacher asks,

"What do you see happening for him next year?"

"Well." I replied. "I see him going to first grade."

What followed was a full minute of silence, the tension in the air being palpable.

"Would that really be the best decision? I spoke to the first grade teacher and she says that the way she does things he would always miss the fun activity because he would probably be completing the required work. The fun activity is contingent on that."

Was this the "fun" activity? Didn't seem like it. When had this conference turned? Wait a minute – back up, lady. Weren't you just talking about what progress he was making and how he seemed like a different child? I was blindsided by this retention discussion, again. Where had the groundwork been laid for this all important discussion? Where was the team decision? Where was the team? Shouldn't she have some support and data to back this up? The only data I saw was a report card that clearly did not in any shape or form support this radical conclusion to my son's kindergarten year. I was beginning to feel like they were determined to retain him this year because I hadn't agreed last year. The mother in me was choking back emotion. The school psychologist in me was not buying it. It wasn't a sound educational suggestion. Had it been, I might have considered it more seriously. If she had support from other school personnel, including the principal of this fine institution, I might have considered the possibility that I was being a "mom" and not using my educational wisdom. At the very least you'd think that someone there would have realized that I needed and expected things to be done correctly from an educational standpoint. She didn't have all her ducks in a row, so to speak, and thus I could not give this bomb shell serious consideration. Of course, being the calm, rational person I am, I heard myself saying that I would consider it and left in an internal huff. Never let them see you sweat.

I began to mull it over in my mind on the way home. I was internally torn. It seemed like the battle lines were being drawn, again. I realized the problem was compounded by the fact I never felt like anyone at this school was my enemy. They were family and I felt bad about their ignorance of educational protocol. I longed for them to know that there was a different way. A way where resources could help students and teachers before retention was considered the only option. Response to Intervention (RTI), a common approach in education, seemed nonexistent at this school, and my son seemed to be one of many victims of its absence. Were there any interventions attempted? If so, none were shared with the worried parent. I wanted to help find an appropriate avenue for his struggles like I had with so many students where I felt retention was not the best solution. I wanted to be a resource and an advocate for this family. The problem was the family was mine and I was not the school psychologist at this school. Again, I reminded myself that I was in the other seat – I was the mom. No one saw me as a school psychologist and no one had the same perception of a school psychology that I had. That reality was being stamped on my heart again. Yes, my hands were tied and I felt powerless and helpless. I have never liked to feel helpless. I would allow myself a few days of self pity and then I needed to find a solution and regain my power as much for my son as for myself and every family I had ever fought for. Once again, if I didn't advocate for my son no one would.

Chapter 11

Going Public

By March of my youngest son's kindergarten year, I was seriously considering the possibility of enrolling him in our local public school district for first grade. I say "seriously considering" because although I knew that was probably the best place for him, my heart still belonged to the private school. We had been there for seven years up until this point and they felt like family. It was comfortable. I knew many families there and was friends with many of the moms. Our kids were friends. Our husbands were friends. I felt like many of the teachers were my friends. It felt comfortable like an old shoe. Still, when the holes keep getting bigger and they are no longer doing the job – it's time for a new pair of shoes. My son needed a better fit. I knew that as a school psychologist. As a mom, I was more torn than I had ever been in my 45 years. It felt like the classic approach-avoidance conflict I had studied about in my Intro Psychology course. Every time I got ready to drive to the public elementary school and register him, I'd inevitably turn around and head home. I kept avoiding what I knew in my head I had to do for my son. The problem was that my heart was not in agreement. Approach-avoidance conflict seemed so interesting in a textbook. This real life situation seemed anything but interesting. Adjectives like chaotic, depressing and heart-wrenching seemed more appropriate for what I was going through that spring of 2006. Yes, this was something I would rather have read about than lived through. But live through it I would – I knew that. I had faith and I knew that alone would see me through this difficult period. I have always believed "If God is for us, who can be against." Above all, I knew that God was for me. He knew what he was doing, even if I felt unsteady and wobbly.

I composed a letter to the kindergarten teacher letting her know that I had decided to enroll him in public school for first grade and beyond. I told her that I was convinced retention was inappropriate and that it was rarely recommended in most schools. It had become increasingly clear that this school was unlike "most schools." I believe to validate my point, I also advised her to read up on the latest studies on retention. She replied within days saying she was sorry to see us go and how much she had enjoyed my youngest son. Yes, for a moment I questioned myself. Everyone had talked about caring for him at this school. They just put very little action behind their talk. With the exception of a few wonderful, experienced teachers most of them did what was easiest for them. I had seen that over and over again. Maybe he'd be o.k? That was the mom in me talking, but the school psychologist knew better. He might actually need a good school psychologist to advocate for him in the coming years. That was something that would never be available to me in this school setting. For the sake of my son, I had to bite the bullet, stick to the course and leave this school. As much as it might hurt in the short-term, the long-term effects on my son's education had more serious implications.

The next order of business was to inform the principal that we would not be re-registering for next year. My oldest son was graduating and going on to a private, costly high school. My next son was due to start sixth grade in the fall. Since our local public middle school started in sixth grade I had asked my middle son if he would like to switch schools also. I knew it was a possibility that some of the experienced teachers who I knew were competent might be retiring soon and I really didn't want to risk whoever might replace them. The judgment of the administration had been brought into question several times over the last few years and my patience was growing thin. The homework load had gotten ridiculous and the principal seemed oblivious to this and other parental concerns. Yes, it seemed like the costs were certainly outweighing the benefits in this school. My second son had always expressed an interest in the public middle school and knew many friends from our neighborhood who attended. I felt certain he wouldn't argue about not having to wear a uniform daily either. Thus it wasn't a total shock when he visited the school, loved it and came home saying, "I want to go to the middle school next year, Mom."

So, in March of that year, with my mind made up, I composed a letter to the principal, informing her that we would not be returning. I addressed many issues that played a role in my decision including her prior lack of responsiveness about many of my concerns. I wrote it, re-wrote it and wrote it again. Did I mention that I tend to obsess about difficult things? When I thought it was just right and said everything I needed to say in a calm, professional manner, I dropped off a copy to her one morning when I took the kids to school. I also dropped off a copy to her supervisor. Being the optimistic person that I am, I felt confident that I would get a reply within a week or two from each of them. My reasoning lay in the fact that private schools rely on tuition to stay afloat and thus hate to lose families, especially full tuition-paying families like ours. Secondly, we had been at the school for seven years, I was an avid supporter of school activities and felt like I was liked there. It felt like they were all "family" and certainly they felt that way about us. I was confident they would set up a meeting where we would discuss my issues and some type of compromise would be reached. Although I was prepared to leave the school if it came to that, I certainly never thought that it would.

We optimistic types see the sunshine, not the rain. We know that everything will work out. We believe people will do the right thing when push comes to shove. We believe most people operate by the same strict principles and ethics we do. I've come to realize that often we set ourselves up to be disappointed by the fallible nature of our species. High expectations often set us up to take a fall. I expected the outcome I wanted. The principal would call me, we would meet, and a compromise would be made. I would end up keeping my boys at this school that felt so comfortable from a mom's perspective. They would see the school psychologist's perspective and change or modify their stance on retention. The massive amounts of homework would quickly be reduced. People in high places would see the error of their ways and learn to be more responsive to parents. Yes, I had it all figured out in my overactive mind. I had written the script and now I just anticipated the players knowing their parts. No revisions were anticipated or necessary. We would all live happily ever after. Optimistic people believe in fairy tales. Every story has a happy ending.

After several weeks of waiting and no contact from either the principal or her supervisor I was beginning to get antsy.

Well, it was a busy time of the year and maybe it was just taking longer than I first anticipated. I waited it out another week and nothing. At this point, I decided that I would write another short note to the principal, inviting her to talk to me about the letter. Yes, I have always been one to take the bull by the horns if a situation warrants that. I was happy when she phoned me a few days later to "set something up to discuss the letter." Good, we could finally get this settled and I could move on with the summer. Fairy tales do come true, it can happen to you.

When I showed up for the meeting that morning, I was hopeful. After all, I had known this principal for a while. She was a reasonable woman. We had actually known each other for over ten years. My children and her children had previously attended the same school. Yes, I felt like we had a history. History should count for something. We had laid the groundwork for an amicable relationship. Another teacher whom I had requested be involved was also present. She had part of the rather unfortunate incident with my son wandering before school and I felt like I had a good relationship with her. I was trying to safeguard against the principal blaming others for us leaving the school. Although many things figured in, her unresponsiveness and lack of leadership was at the helm of my decision. I was hoping she would realize that and maybe alter her future dealings with parents.

The meeting started off cordial enough and, in retrospect, stayed that way throughout. I tried to stay in the constructive criticism mode since I have always felt like being nice accomplishes more than yelling and blaming people. Being the prepared, organized type, I brought a notebook with a rough outline of the points I wanted to address at the school that were factors in my decision to leave. It seemed to me like the principal had a logical explanation for everything. Rather than admitting that, yes, I did have some valid points she proceeded to justify everything I cited. She also totally ignored and brushed off many of my well-thought out points. Not exactly what I expected. I have always thought life is a learning experience and no one individual knows it all. Not so in this case. She came across as knowing it all and assumed the "excellent" reputation of her school should speak for itself. The problem was that few, if any, people on the inside of this school thought it was excellent. No institution is perfect. Every institution can benefit from improvements and an objective point of view. The whole experience was disappointing. It appeared that she really did not care if we left or not. She, as the administrator, never once said, "What can we do to get you to stay?" "How can we work together for the benefit of your sons?" These are things that are routinely discussed in every school I have ever worked in when a family decides to leave. Apparently this school was far above that very productive attitude. It was unexpected and hurtful, but not altogether surprising. Putting on blinders seemed to be a pattern here. If the principal had been more responsive and open in the first place, it never would have come to this.

So, I left that March day resolved to put it all in God's hands. If we were meant to stay, then someone would contact me over the summer and we could negotiate. If we were meant to leave, then I would deal with it somehow. I have never been big on changes but sometimes they are so necessary, and this might be the only way to get the educational services my son needed and deserved, as did every student who was struggling in that school. Yes, I would do anything for my children and their well-being.

Summer began and so did our regular summer routine, which included swim team in the mornings, lots of outdoor activities during the day and swim meets two nights a week. Summer has always been my favorite season of the year. It is warm, relaxed and generally very easy-going. Maybe the fact that I was born in California explains my love of the sun and warm weather. Summer means beaches, picnics and taking it easy, and although we do generally schedule some activities, the sheer luxury of not having to transport four kids to school activities and pack lunches makes it quite enjoyable. As the summer progressed, I was tempted to phone the supervisor and see if he had received the copy of the letter. Tempted, but not totally convinced I should do that. I really felt like the ball was in his court and he would contact me eventually. He must just be busy or out of town. The idea that a supervisor of an educational establishment would totally ignore a "customer" never entered my mind. By the end of the summer, when I was still waiting for a response, it began to occur to me that I wasn't going to get one. At first it seemed rude, but then it made me angry – very angry. As a family who had been in this school for seven years, didn't we deserve a response? That would have been common courtesy, not to mention a very Christian response. At the very least, some acknowledgement of my concerns might have been nice. Were they that secure in their membership at the school that they could afford to ignore members? I was insulted and angry but mostly extremely disappointed. Disappointed in an institution I had devoted my adult life to. I was disappointed in people who professed to "care" but really did not live up to that claim. If I was hesitant to leave before – this really sealed the deal for me. Certainly if they did not care about me and my family, why should I hang on? Seemed like God in his infinite wisdom was sending me the clear message I was so desperately looking for. Yes, it was time to move on to greener pastures. I craved pastures where maybe people really lived the Christianity I had always embraced. The hypocrisy of it all was upsetting and threw me for a loop, but I resolved to do what God was asking me to do. He knew what was best for me and my family and obviously he was telling us to leave. It was a tough call, but I've always trusted God to lead me where he wants me. Intellectually, I knew it was the only decision, emotionally it would probably be a bumpy road.

The only consolation that fall lay in the fact that several other families who were friends of ours had also made the difficult decision to leave the school for similar reasons. Curiously enough, most of them were in education. Did anyone at that school see a pattern here? The reality is, to see a pattern, you have to be looking for one and realize you need help. Ignorance is a wonderful insulator. Likewise, other people going through the same thing and validating your points can be a much needed blessing. I'm sure this is where the expression "misery loves company" comes in. Yes, I certainly could use the company on this trip.

So in fall of 2006, my two youngest sons started in public school. I was thrilled we didn't have to mess with the whole uniform ordeal that we normally went through at the beginning of every school year. Determining who needs what in the uniform department every July is exhausting with four children. The measuring, ordering and making sure everything is authorized by the strict guidelines of the school can be time consuming. Once my final decision had been reached, I quickly bundled up all our uniforms and gave them to another family in the school who I thought could use them. "Out of sight, out of mind" is another platitude that has worked well in my life. If you box up the physical reminders, you won't think about that place anymore. That's a good theory anyway. Needless to say, the boys did not miss the uniforms one bit. Actually my youngest had never been in a uniform since kindergartners were not required to wear them so he didn't appreciate not having to wear a uniform the way his brother did.

Standing out at that new bus stop with my youngest was a different experience. Of course I knew all of the "public school" families from our neighborhood, but the bus stop was a different location and came an hour earlier than the private school bus. I think in most districts the public school children are bused first and then the private school children. This is inevitably why many private schools start later. My children's old school started at 9:00 and the new one started at 8:00. I found out rather quickly that this early time start was wonderful if you were a working mother. Rather than pay for "before care" as I had done for many years at the previous school, I could merely put my youngest on the bus and be on my way to my school. His brother's bus came an hour later since he was in middle school, but he was twelve then and capable of getting himself breakfast and on the bus independently. We actually joked the first few months that he would be doing his own "before care" at home and saving me money in the long run.

The first few weeks went very smoothly. We had met his first grade teacher at a visitation day before school started and I shared some background on my son with her. I explained that this was his first year and that he did not know many of the students. We went from a school where there were approximately 48 students in kindergarten to a school where there were over 300 in first grade. We lived in an excellent school system and thus there was a constant flux of families moving to our area for the schools. This new setting was somewhat of a culture shock for me in particular, but my son seemed to take it all in stride. I had a difficult time even finding the first grade hallway many times when I entered the school. I'm not generally good with directions anyway and I longed for the color coded lines they put on the floor in some airports. If I could have followed the yellow line to the first grades, I would have been fine.

When conference time rolled around in November I was eager to sit with my son's teacher and get some feedback on how he was doing. The first conferences in most schools are mandatory and I took comfort in this. I was more than curious to see how this new, presumably more heterogeneous setting would affect my son. His teacher had many wonderful things to say about my son right off the bat. He was "very considerate" of the other children and "well mannered." He was "happy" most of the time and showed "good cooperation." I almost had tears in my eyes when I heard her rattle off his good traits. They were not as hard to find for her as for previous teachers, apparently. She did say he was "having difficulty warming up to other children." The first few weeks apparently he just sat to the side at circle time and did not want to participate. However, she did add that this had all changed in the last month and he was joining in more now. I shared that I had noticed this pattern with my youngest and in his older brother as well. They prefer to observe for a while before they dive right in. His teacher, by the way, did not label this as a "problem" or "lack of socialization", as some other teachers had. No label was attached to this behavior, she merely reported what she saw. She said his reading was behind, but she had already hooked him up with an Intervention Specialist who would take him in a small group and help with that. It seemed like they were doing an intervention without me having to ask for it. What a concept. These people really seemed to understand early childhood education and truly helping children to succeed. I was very curious about the whole retention issue so near the end of our wonderful conference I asked,

"Do you think he belongs in first grade or should I have retained him? You certainly have an opinion after having him for nine weeks."

What came next was the sweetest music I had heard in years.

"Retained? Certainly not, he is right where he should be. He is a very bright boy and will do fine. I have no doubts."

With that wonderful news, I quickly swallowed the emotion rising in my throat, thanked her and rose to leave the room.

"I think it is very important that we keep in close contact on how we can work together to help him be the best he can be," she added as I left.

"So do I, and thank you so much for all your help. He is in the right place – I know that now."

And I did. This wonderful woman had set me at ease with some very simple positive traits she saw shining in my son. Things I had always known were there but were brushed aside like they didn't matter in the scheme of developmental benchmarks like coloring fast and tying shoes. I said a silent prayer as I left that "public" school on that fall day. A "public" school, where prayer was not a part of the daily routine, but where people were shining examples of the Christian values I had always embraced. People truly treated others as they would like to be treated. I was grateful for excellent schools with resources and teachers who believed in each child's ability to succeed, wherever their skills were. Yes, he was in the right place. He would be fine. This I knew for sure for the first time in two years and that realization brought tears of profound joy for all that would be. God in his infinite wisdom had led us to this place.

As my son progressed through that school year, he became more comfortable in his new surroundings and I became more comfortable as a parent taking him there. I did end up having him evaluated for Attention Deficit Disorder privately at the end of that school year. He continued to be distracted and off task often and, after numerous conversations with his teacher, I decided it was time to address these issues. He did receive the diagnosis of Attention Deficit Disorder-Inattentive Type at the end of first grade. That simply meant he took longer to complete some tasks, and needed re-directing often, not that he lacked intelligence or could not succeed with his age peers. It simply meant putting some accommodations in place which this excellent school district was willing to do. He received a 504 Plan which is a legal document for children with ADD who need accommodations in the regular classroom to succeed.

I sometimes think I had a harder time adjusting to changing schools than either of my boys. I know that sounds silly, but I attended private schools for sixteen years and had worked in them for fifteen up to that point. They were a part of my life and to have them suddenly plucked away through circumstances I could not control was devastating to me. On top of that, my two older children who had graduated from the school didn't really understand why I transferred their brothers. I took some comfort in the fact that I continued to work in the same private school that had employed me for the past three years. I was surrounded by parents and students and continued to advocate for them and the services they needed at my school. There, I knew I made a difference and would continue to. This was a wonderful private school and there are many. I had much more control in that setting than I ever did in the school setting we left. That was the unfortunate reality and one I would have to come to grips with. As comforting as it was at times to continue to work in that environment, it was also bitter-sweet on occasion. My emotions seemed to be on a pendulum. Some days I was so grateful for my son's new educational setting and some days I longed for things to be the way they were before – familiar and predictable, with a dash of daily prayer thrown in.

I have come to embrace what I have heard for years. "We can never really understand another's journey until we have walked in their shoes." Many will never understand how difficult this journey was for me. I truly do not understand it myself. Many have left a private school without a glance back. Many have advised me over the years to just "forget about it and move on." That is difficult to do when you truly love an institution and know it could be better with a little effort in the right direction. Better for your children and for every student and parent who walks through the doors and lays down their hard earned money for an excellent education. An education where every family matters and people in administration humble themselves to admit they don't know everything there is to know. "Excellence" is more than a word. The dictionary defines it as being, "superior" and "better than others." In an excellent school setting changes are embraced instead of avoided at all costs. In an excellent school setting every child matters and every parent is heard and respected. Above all, people humble themselves and admit they don't know everything. In an excellent school setting, supervisors listen and respond when parents have concerns.

When you are an advocate for students' rights, it is part of your being, not something you can just forget and lay aside. Moving on can be the most difficult thing you've ever done, but move on we must. We can never go back, only forward, and with help from God as well as some earthly angels who walked beside me, I would.

Chapter 12

Sing Your Own Special Song

When my youngest began second grade, I began contemplating a difficult decision in my professional life. I came to realize that it was in my destiny to leave a company that had employed me over a span of twenty years. I realized that I no longer agreed with the way they conducted their business. A huge part of this decision stemmed from my inability to access appropriate services for my son when he needed them at his previous school. The company I worked for supplied school psychology services at this school. I had known for years that their services were less than adequate at many schools but now their lack of services and accountability had directly impacted my life and the life of my son. That reality cut into my soul. The choice was clear. I could no longer support a company that did not support children and families in the best possible way. For whatever reasons, services were not available when we needed them. Teachers were not knowledgeable about these services and if they were did not have access to these services. Administrators chose to look the other way. People did not advocate for interventions for children the way I always had. It was wrong and while I admit I have made mistakes in my life, I have always chosen right over wrong. That is the bottom line. I have never supported doing what is ethically and morally against my conscience, and thus I knew I had to quit. If I wasn't part of the solution, I would be part of the problem. It was an inevitable, yet uncomfortable decision.

I knew I would have to give the principal advance notice of my decision to leave at the end of the school year. Although I would have loved to continue to work at the school I was assigned to, I realized this might not be possible. Private schools contract for school psychology services and I knew my employer had the contract for this school for at least the next few years. The principal's hands were probably tied. Hence when I approached her about this decision, I wasn't feeling too hopeful that she could provide any solution. She assured me that she would be very disappointed if I left, but would not be able to keep me except through the company I currently worked for. That was predictable, but upsetting nevertheless. I have always believed my dad's mantra "where there is a will, there is a way" and it seemed like there should be a way. I could not accept that there was no way. I was good for this school and I belonged here. Somehow it could work, I knew it and would leave no stone unturned. Did I mention that besides being optimistic, I am stubborn? After spending many sleepless nights trying desperately to arrive at a solution to my dilemma and coming up blank, I approached the principal again. Again, she assured me that I was the best school psychologist she had ever worked with and she valued me immensely.

"Couldn't you just stick it out for the school?"

I thought about that for about a half a second.

"No, I can't – it just isn't me."

My mother and father raised us to be true to ourselves and to do the right thing. To stick to our core values and ethics even if it was the hardest thing we ever did. I wasn't about to "stick it out" even though I truly loved this school and knew

I was valued. Continuing to work for this company meant I endorsed their practices, which I did not. I had been "comfortable" working for them for years but when I needed them for my son, they were not there. I had witnessed them letting other people down over the years but their latest incompetence affected my life and directly impacted my son. I could not stick it out anymore. Many people would not understand this, which ate away at me for a while. My professional and personal lives were so interwoven. The rights of students in the educational setting which I believed in so strongly were not being honored in the best way. Many individuals who professed to have children and families' best interests in mind were consistently coming up short. I longed to shout my reasoning and the injustice I had endured at the top of my lungs but knew I could not. In the end I alone understood my reasoning which is all that really matters. Actually, a few close friends provided a shoulder and empathized as best they could, and for that I am eternally grateful. I knew I was doing the right thing, as uncertain as my professional future was. Emotionally it was difficult, intellectually it was sound. This was the second time in the span of a few years I would have to sacrifice emotions for an intellectually sound decision. I wasn't sure I was up for the challenge alone. But then, we are never really alone if we have faith. I was confident faith would see me through. It always has.

I made up my mind that I would go into private practice in school psychology. Yes, I was destined to advocate for children and families because of my training and because I knew first hand what having two sons with learning challenges was all about. Once I have a plan, I go for it. That was another thing my dad taught us. Make a plan and put it into action.

You can achieve anything you set your mind to. He not only spoke it, he lived it. I knew I had to obtain licensure through the State Board of Psychology to set up a private practice. I had always been licensed through the State Department of Education, which is what is necessary to work as a school psychologist in schools in Ohio. To work outside of schools as a school psychologist, an individual needs a license through the State Board of Psychology. Many people who work in schools have both. I had heard horror stories over the years about how difficult the exam was. There was apparently a written part and an oral exam administered by licensed psychologists at the Board Office in Columbus. The thought of an oral exam terrified me beyond words. While I think I am a confident speaker, the thought of being quizzed orally has never thrilled me. Actually, I'm not sure I had ever taken an oral exam up until that point and I must say it seemed as appealing as being thrown into an ocean with live sharks circling. Actually maybe sharks that haven't eaten in a month or two is a better comparison. Yes, I felt sure this would not be a pleasant experience.

As frightening as the whole ordeal seemed, I knew it was necessary to achieve the goals I had set for myself. I have always been very goal orientated and never let fear stop me. Fear is powerful and has sometimes threatened to steer me off course but I always re-group and get back on track. I would conquer it, as I always had in the past. I truly believe "if you don't stand for something, you'll fall for anything." Yes, it was time to take a stand in my professional and personal life. Taking a stand included taking an oral exam and hence, it would have to be done. I would study and prepare and I would obtain that license which I needed to begin a new,

wonderful chapter in my life. The times they were a changing
and I was ready to climb that mountain that lay before me.

I began to explore exactly what becoming licensed would
entail in the summer of 2007. The criteria were threefold. I
would have to take a Praxis Exam which was a standardized,
written exam which basically encompassed anything I had
studied to prepare for my job as a school psychologist, anything I used in the job daily and legal matters related to
school psychology. Secondly, I would need to obtain three letters of recommendations from licensed school psychologists
and thirdly, I would have to take the oral exam in Columbus,
where the State Board of Psychology was located.

The first step was to prepare for the Praxis Exam. I found
out though a website that this exam was given three times a
year. I decided to sign up for the first exam, which was in October. I decided three months was plenty of time to prepare
and dragging it out any further would just increase the anxiety I was beginning to feel about the whole process. I ordered
a review book that was offered at the time of registration and
set about the task of studying. This task seemed daunting. I
was the mother of four children ages 16, 15, 12 and 7 and was
due to start back working at my school three days a week.
How would I find time to study? Did I mention that my husband has always traveled extensively for his job and I was by
myself with the kids often? I also hadn't actually studied for
anything since graduate school which was about eighteen
years prior. I was a middle aged woman who had to find time
for extensive study. What had I taken on? Maybe I should just
scrap the whole plan and stay where I was. The thought did
enter my mind , but it fled just as quickly. No, Mary, you are

sticking to this plan. It is, after all, what needs to be done – end of story.

Trying desperately to squash defeating thoughts, I made a very specific plan. Yes, a plan for success was called for. I decided to study at the library as many days a week as I could for at least three hours at a time. When school resumed I would study on my days off when the kids were in school. On the weekends I would study on one of the two days and leave the kids with my husband. As much as he traveled during the week, he was always home on weekends. My husband questioned why I had to study at the library. He just didn't get it. Most mothers trying to study for something so important probably would. Trying to study at home with four kids, assorted friends, television noises and various hysterical calls for "Mom!" at all hours can be self-defeating to say the least. I have always believed in stacking the cards in my favor, and going to the library, which was relatively distraction-free, set me up for success not failure. Secondly, if things didn't turn out the way I planned, I had only myself to blame and my lack of discipline. I could not, would not later say "Oh, I didn't pass because my kids kept bugging me when I was trying to study." No this was all on my shoulders. Whatever the outcome, I alone would accept responsibility.

I remember receiving the "Study Guide" in the mail and being so excited. This was it – my key to freedom and private practice! Yes, I could do this, I was ready, I was excited, I was determined. I sat down to browse through the first few sections of the book the day it arrived. Like a small child looking at new bedroom furniture after sharing a room with big sis year after year. This book meant independence, freedom, a new start. I flipped open the cover full of anticipation for all that would be. Wow! Glancing at the table of contents, anticipation turned to dread. Half of these topics I was sure we had never covered in graduate school. Or maybe my middle aged, brain had merely forgotten them? What could have caused this memory lapse? Was it hormones, childbirth, life with peanut butter and jelly? Could I get a passing grade? Yes, of course I could! Positive thinking. "Where there's a will, there's a way." "When the going gets tough, the tough get going." All of these fraternal messages bombarded my dormant brain at that precise moment. I am woman hear me roar. I think I can, I think I can, choo-choo. Yes, I would have to include The Little Engine in my study routine. Lord knows my son wouldn't mind hearing it for the 1059th time.

So the first time I set out for the library, study guide and reference materials in hand, I was anxious but determined. I knew in my heart it could be done but I was slightly overwhelmed and wasn't sure even how to begin. With students and adults alike, I find that this is often the biggest obstacle to success. How do I even begin to accomplish this thing I want so badly? Sometimes the task to get us to a certain goal seems so overwhelming that many people throw in the towel. For the first ten minutes I just stared at the material. How do I start? There is so much to cover in a few short months.

I think at that point, I literally slapped myself in the face and said out loud, "Quitting is not an option – you are doing this. Believe it – achieve it!" There was too much fuel behind the fire not to. Positive self-talk has always helped move me forward and thus I pulled it out of my bag of tricks when I needed it most.

I started by breaking the material into sections, outlining what I would study in each session. This is the key to any daunting task. Yes, manageable parts always makes the whole seem less overwhelming and the mountain easier to climb. It was time to use all the study techniques I had been spouting to students for years. Now, I was the student and I needed a coach and a cheerleader. I would have to be both. This is a life lesson I have learned to embrace. If you can't find a coach and a cheerleader, be your own. No one is more invested in your situation and the outcome than you are. You will thank the coach and ultimately they will be promoted later.

I had a plan, an outline and I had notecards. I was all set. I studied for three hours that first day, making sure to take breaks and treat myself several times throughout the session. I was fortunate enough to find a new, modern library near our home. It had many quiet areas for studying as well as a "Café" for snacking in the front. I allowed myself several ten minute breaks when I arrived at a logical stopping point in studying. Yes, there is nothing like a latte and a cookie to propel you onward! Keeps the blood sugar up, too, which is necessary in absorbing knowledge. Feeling refreshed and re-newed, I was ready to begin the next session. I refused to let myself get tired and worn out which would inevitably lead to the "poor pity me" syndrome. No, that definitely was not in the plan. I had no time for pity and self-defeating thoughts. Success involves careful planning, strategic maneuvering and of course – coffee! I went home feeling hopeful and actually looking forward to the next study session. I decided to keep all of my study materials in my car so that I would be equipped to stop by the library whenever a block of time arose. Being prepared is another necessary ingredient of success.

As the months progressed and school resumed, I found it easier and easier to study. "Easy" may not be the right word here. It was "do-able" – that's it. I felt more and more confident that it was do-able. A middle aged woman with four kids and a husband who traveled 50% of the time could set a career goal for herself and accomplish it. I would be the living proof! I was making progress weekly towards this very lofty goal I had set for myself. I felt sure my father was smiling down on me, knowing that his little girl was climbing the mountain and would make it to the top to carry the toys over to all of the children waiting – choo-choo! So, I prodded on, every Sunday afternoon heading off to the library with my books, study guide, notecards and above all – confidence. I was confident it could be done. Nothing else was acceptable in this scenario. I had told too many people I was working on obtaining my license in school psychology. This fact alone stirred me on. I was being watched, I was accountable and above all, I did not want to be embarrassed by not passing! Yes, telling too many people will do that to you. In retrospect, that might have been a mistake, but it kept me on the right track. The track dreams are made of.

There were days when I just did not "feel" like going to the library. Days when it would have been easier to stay home and lay around, read a book, play with the kids or just vegetate in front of that big black box where we all seek out mindless refuge. Generally, feelings get in the way of goals and success. I knew this intellectually, having studied many successful people. I refused to let "feelings" get in the way of my goal. It would have been very easy to and I'll admit to being weak on occasion and loitering in the garage, books in hand. But on those days I asked myself the all important question.

Who really cares if I study or not? Not my family. They would love me no matter what I did. To them I was just mom, who happened to work in a school. The jury was still out on how much enjoyment they derived from that. Would my husband care if I studied? Probably not, I'd be home more on Sundays to watch the older kids and keep the youngest occupied and maybe he wouldn't be asked to start dinner once in a while. The only one who would truly suffer would be me, the one who had started all of this business in the first place. Why had I started this? I had to remind myself often when weariness threatened to consume me. I started it because it was the right thing to do. The only thing – I knew that deep in my gut. That alone would sustain me. Yes, I must persist towards my one, true mission, for myself as much as for families and students who needed support.

When that October test date began to approach, I felt confident that I was ready. Confidence rolled up in nerves. Nerves speckled with confidence. Yes, the two seemed to be tightly interwoven at this point. The written test was given at a state university about an hour from our house. I drove there early one Saturday morning and completed the two hour exam with other people in education. To my delight, I found out six weeks later that I passed. On to the next step, the oral exam in Columbus.

That exam was scheduled in early February and I again, I had to study diligently for about three months to prepare. The night before the big exam in Columbus, I had to drive two hours to the state capital. The exam was scheduled for 8:00 a.m. and thus I elected to drive down the night before and get a hotel room, so that I could be relaxed and ready in the morning and avoid leaving our house at 5:00. This way I could also review my notes in the room the night before free of family distractions.

Despite having tried several times to determine exactly how long the oral exam would be, no one seemed able to give me a clear answer. The people at the State office said "anywhere from one to two hours." People I knew who had actually taken the exam said, "It's never more than thirty minutes – tops." That seemed to be a contradiction and one that had me slightly on edge. I like to know precisely what to expect going into a situation. I like to be prepared. There is a huge difference between thirty minutes and two hours in my book. Precisely an hour and a half. Quite a few questions can be packed into an hour and a half. The only saving grace was that all of the written literature I had seen that described the exam did outline the four areas to be covered. Apparently each area had one question that was asked. I guess that narrowed it down. Maybe some people just took longer to clarify the answer. Yes, that must be it.

So that February evening, I said good-bye to my husband and the kids and headed to Columbus. As luck would have it, I left on Valentine's Day. That's o.k., it's never been a big occasion in my life. A card and a kiss good-bye and I was on my way. It was about a two and a half hour drive so I set out in the early evening, figuring I'd get there in plenty of time to check into the hotel, review my note cards and get a good night's sleep before the exam the next morning. I made up my mind to try and relax on the way there and not review the notes in my head. That is my tendency – to get all worked up over things but I made a conscious decision not to let myself. Yes, a little Celine Dion and Amy Grant music was just the ticket. If there's one thing I believe in for myself and others, it is the calming effect of music. Music soothes the nerves and brings peace and tranquility to any situation.

Arriving at the hotel at 8:00, after grabbing a fast-food burger on the road for dinner I was ready for a quick review. My older sister called as I was getting ready to study and inquired if I knew how to get to the building for the exam in the morning. Columbus is a confusing city and knowing my lack of direction, I was grateful for the assistance. Once we determined the best route in the morning, I hung up quickly. Normally I like idle chit-chat but not the night before an important exam when my stomach is in knots. No, idle chit-chat had no place in this hotel room. I reviewed my note cards for a couple of hours, determined I knew them backwards and forwards and decided to try and get some sleep. I use the word "try" because ever since I was a little girl I have trouble sleeping the night before a big event. What qualifies as a "big event" is different for every person, of course. My "big events" seem to be anything I define as mildly threatening and unpredictable. They can be as mundane as the first day in a new situation to a life changing exam – like this one. I remember as a five-year old crying before kindergarten and not wanting to get out of the car. It was only after some bribing from my father that my parents were able to extract me, not without some kicking and screaming, as I recall. A similar incident occurred at the beginning of high school. I'm sure my own struggles are what attracted me to the field of psychology in the first place. I have come to realize, after years of self-analysis, a hazard of the profession, that I have an anxious personality. As much as I have learned to recognize it and use techniques to manage it, I inevitably have difficulty sleeping the night before a major event like this one.

After lying awake for what seemed like hours, counting sheep, thinking of pleasant, non-threatening events like Disney World, and numerous other techniques I know to relax myself, I must have finally succumbed to sleep. I awoke around five thirty and rolled over numerous times trying to go back to sleep. The wake-up call wasn't scheduled until six-thirty and I desperately wanted to rest more – but to no avail. Another symptom of anxiety I've learned to live with is waking up early on the day of a big event. Actually, this can be a good thing at times. I'm never late for important things. I'm always raring to go and have plenty of time to review my notes before a test – a study technique that insures success.

After having a light breakfast, I headed to the car to drive the few blocks to the exam. Funny how a few blocks in a big city like Columbus can take you thirty minutes to maneuver. This was partly due to the fact that Columbus has a lot of one-way streets. Just when you see where you want to go and attempt to turn, it becomes obvious you can't. Frustration takes on a whole new meaning when you drive in Columbus. Whoever designed the city undoubtedly did so with a lot of revenue from traffic tickets in mind. With the design of the city in mind, I actually allowed forty minutes for the trip. Even without one way streets, I am not good with directions. Yes, map reading skill is definitely not something I inherited. Numerous people, including my husband, have tried to instruct me over the years but they have had little success and ended up convinced that it was a lost cause. That part of my brain just does not function well. Give me words over lines and curves any day. The drive was supposed to take ten minutes. Figuring in time to make wrong turns, parking and a bathroom break, forty minutes seemed about right. "The early bird catches the worm" is also one of my life mantras. Lateness screams of low priority or poor planning, both of which are counterproductive to success.

Arriving at the test cite with ten minutes to spare even after the bathroom stop, I was told that the examiner "is not ready for you yet, please be seated for a few minutes." Darn, darn, darn! I'm sure some people would have liked this moment to collect their thoughts. My problem is that in these situations I am prone to collecting doubt, worry and anxiety. I would much rather have been herded into the exam room so that all of that knowledge didn't have a chance to leak out of my tightly packed brain. I inevitably start reviewing information in my mind, can't remember some crucial fact and begin to doubt my ability to succeed. Knowing this scenario from past events, I was determined not to let this happen and calmly began self-talk. "You're ready, you know you're ready, you know this stuff. You will pass. It will only be a few minutes now and you will be a Licensed School Psychologist. Believe it. Believe it. Believe it."

"Mrs. Shafer, the examiner is ready for you now."

"What?" I managed, breaking through my trance like recitation.

"The examiner will see you now – and good luck."

I was lead to a large conference room at the end of a winding hallway. At least I took some comfort in the fact that the secretary had said "the examiner." That inevitably meant that there wasn't a panel of ten psychologists ready to chew me up and spit me out. Yes, I felt sure I could handle whatever one mere mortal could throw at me. After all "I am strong, I am invincible, I am woman!" Yes, there she was. It was one very professional looking woman alright and she rose to shake my hand, introducing herself as I entered the room. She began by asking where I drove from, how the directions were, etc. Small talk, chit-chat. Nice idea but let's get to it shall we? Maybe my one word answers and the ringing of my hands gave her the subtle hint.

"O.K, shall we begin?"

Sounds great to me, girlfriend. Or maybe Doctor Girlfriend is more appropriate.

Ever get that nauseating, "get me out of here" feeling in the pit of your stomach? That's what happened to me when the first question was posed. It was something so minor in the scheme of all the material I had studied that I barely recognized it from the material. The kind of question where immediately following the exam you grab your study guide and feverishly hunt for it – positively sure it isn't even listed in the review material. Actually, I did remember seeing it there, it just seemed so unimportant in the vast array of my "school psychology" knowledge that I was sure they would "never ask that." It went something like, "What are the five different titles a school psychologist can be addressed as and under what circumstances is each title given?" Let me see – the first one that pops into my head immediately is "naïve fool" This dubious title refers to a person who thought certain information was too mundane to ever be asked and thus is raking her brain for some semi-logical answer and looking grossly unprepared. Actually I knew two-three answers right away but the other two – no clue! This is when I began to be creative and think back on any title I ever heard professors called in the school psychology program twenty years ago and any title I had ever heard anyone I'd come across professionally referred to since. Exhausting those rather quickly I resorted to,

Did I say_____?" "How many is that?" and a barrage or other stall techniques as I silently prayed for divine intervention. Yes, God has always seen me through the rough spots and now I beckoned him with every ounce of my being.

As I verbally fumbled around, praying I could stay afloat, I heard the examiner say,

"You are doing fine, relax, you only need one more and we will move on."

This woman was a Godsend. She was actually helping me instead of writing me off as someone who was not ready to be licensed by The State Department of Psychology! What an angel. She knew what I needed to boost my confidence and she provided it. Gratitude didn't begin to describe it. I was ready to write her into my will based on this simple gesture of kindness. Miraculously, I did come up with the last title and we did in fact move on to the next category.

As I recall, there was one other time when I was unsure of a response but somehow I managed to pull it off. I'm not sure I could have if the examiner had been rigid, unfeeling or just plain mean. Her attitude set the tone for what could have been a very tense situation. She enabled me to succeed and bring forth the knowledge I knew I had. Yes, for the most part we psychologists are an empathetic breed and I've never appreciated it more than I did that day. Near the end of the exam she even added,

"O.K., just one more answer and you will be a Licensed School Psychologist. Take a deep breath and take what is yours."

Wow, what an empowering statement that was! After my well-thought out response she stood up, reached across the table to shake my hand and proclaimed,

"Congratulations, you are now a Licensed School Psychologist!"

Every ounce of my being wanted to jump across the table and hug her, but I held myself back from fear of loosing my license as quickly as I had gained it. I do remember asking,

"Do people scream, because I feel like screaming."

She just smiled and replied,

"Some have – go for it."

I did let out a little "Whoopee", but when it comes right down to it I know when professionalism is called for, and this seemed like an appropriate time. I wasn't about to risk all I had worked for. No, the hoopla could wait until I got home. Bring on the celebratory dinner!

After some small talk with the examiner, she instructed me to "return to the main office where they will have some paperwork for you to complete the process." There the secretary told me that normally it takes a few weeks to actually receive your license but she could expedite that and I could take it home today if I had a few minutes to wait. Sure, no problem. I'd rather wait a few minutes then have to go home and sweat it out daily, waiting and wondering if the mail would bring this much anticipated piece of paper. She then disappeared and I waited, and waited and waited. I'm sure everyone has been in this situation where "a few minutes" turns into thirty minutes which turns into forty-five, and gradually approaches an hour. The odd thing was that I didn't see this woman again during the whole waiting period. It was a busy office and people were coming and going continuously. Other secretaries were passing in and out busily completing their assigned tasks but no sign of the women I was waiting for – ever so patiently. After about fifteen minutes of this, a young man in a suit entered and announced that he was "scheduled to take the licensing exam for school psychology." After he took a seat next to mine I casually mentioned that I had just completed it and said, "good luck." After wiping his hands on his expensive looking suit and cracking his knuckles he mumbled, "Yeah, thanks, I guess." His downward glance and lack of eye contact spoke volumes. He was obviously in the "just leave me alone – I have to get this over with" phase. I knew that feeling all too well and so stifled any further chit-chat. Actually if it had been a woman I might have been inclined to offer more commentary but, even in the best of circumstances, most men I know are not big on idle chit-chat in any form. No, they are generally very task-orientated. Get the job done and move on to the next one.

After about twenty minutes, clearly the duration for "a few minutes" I began to wonder, what was taking this woman so long. Surely they weren't thinking of revoking my license after it had just been bestowed upon me? Maybe the examiner had discovered that one of my answers was wrong after all. Maybe they dug up that mild rule infraction from my past that disqualified me on an ethical technicality. Yes, that must be it. Suddenly the time I was twelve and left the counter at Woolworth's without paying for my milkshake flashed through my head. At the time I thought I was clearly justified as the waitress had reluctantly served my friend and I because of our young ages. When she didn't return with the check we had requested, Laura had coaxed me into casually walking out. Somehow "it serves her right" had seemed logical at the time. That incident had haunted my conscience for years. There were several times years later when I almost drove back and paid the bill, to ease my conscience as well as re-claim my "good girl" status. Now it was threatening to destroy my career. Yes, that one rebellious act thirty-five years ago had finally come to light. It was time to pay for the sins of my youth. Hadn't the nuns told us that "God never forgets"? Yes, an active imagination can be a blessing and a curse all wrapped up in one!

After thirty minutes and still no secretary, I began to think maybe she had taken a coffee break and forgotten all about me. Was that possible? Could someone just leave like that in the middle of doing something so vital to my future? Then again, this inevitably was something she did every day. Processing a License was part of her daily routine. Did she just set it down somewhere in the middle of a caffeine craving and rush out to Starbucks? Who knew? Certainly not me, but I was beginning to get impatient, aggravated and annoyed. What had been sheer bliss forty minutes ago was quickly turning to frustration, aggravation and anxiety all rolled up into a big mess of emotional turmoil. Did I mention that an active imagination can quickly turn to panic? Just as I was beginning to wonder if I should ask another secretary about her whereabouts before I worked myself up into a coronary, I glanced up and the mystery woman was strolling into the office like she didn't have a care in the world. "Here you go," she said, as she handed me the license and some other papers. Not even a hint of explanation of why the few minutes had turned into an hour. Relax, take a deep breath. Don't let this pet peeve get the best of you. Slow-moving, unmotivated people – difficult to understand on even my best day. But, I reminded myself silently, this is one of my ultimate best days. I have my School Psychology License, I can start my practice and better yet, I can leave Columbus – a very busy, confusing city.

As I headed out of the building and towards the lot where I had parked, I silently prayed it would still be there. In my nervousness to get to the exam, I had parked in an area that I wasn't sure was authorized. I couldn't get into the garage I wanted to park in due to the one-way street dilemma and was running late at that point. I haphazardly pulled into a spot that seemed to indicate "tow away zone." Actually, it clearly indicated that but being the positive, punctual person I am I just locked up the car and ran for it. What's a girl to do? Did I mention I was driving my husband's car? That fact alone led me to saying not one prayer but the whole rosary on the way back to my spot. To say that my husband would never understand parking in a tow away zone is a gross understatement. It would probably rank right up there with the time I backed into his car in the driveway. He had arrived home early from a business trip and I totally forgot it was there. "Why didn't you look back before you pulled out? He innocently inquired. "Well, if you were home more often, it never would have happened." That's what you call rationalization in psychology. Or maybe "desperate housewife syndrome." In any event, having a car towed away in Columbus did not seem like the best scenario and one I was sure not looking forward to facing. I just did not want to make that phone call to my husband if it came down to that. "The good news is I passed the Licensing Exam. The bad new is your car was towed and I need you to figure out what to do with the kids and drive down here and get me." Did I mention that Columbus is a two and a half hour drive from Cleveland? No, this would not be good by any stretch of the imagination. This might be a good time to pray again.

Miraculously, as I approached the lot and peered around the corner where I had left the car, it was still there! Thank you God! You saved me again. Clearly I had used up my monthly share of miracles all in one day. I quickly surveyed the windshield for the dreaded ticket and it was empty! What a stroke of luck, faith or a shortage of policemen in Columbus. Whatever the reason, it was a gift, for sure! With that worry behind me I quickly unlocked the door, jumped in and sped out of there with a vengeance. I didn't need anyone spotting me leaving that space at this point either. Go speed racer, go!

Heading home on the highway my spirits were soaring. Celine Dion never sounded so good. Actually my singing with her never sounded so good either. I was flying so high I convinced myself that if Sony offered me a record deal tomorrow I'd be a worthy contender for a Grammy. Yes, I was feeling that good. A new School Psychology License and avoiding a ticket and/or and impounded car to boot. The slogan I had come to love on my t shirt "Life is Good" took on a whole new meaning. I called my husband, told him the news and gave him an estimate of when I would be arriving home. It's funny how a long drive always seems shorter when the anticipated event is over. It seemed like I got home in record time.

It was dinner time when I walked in the door. The kids were waiting for me, the house was a mess and there was no food in sight. There's no place like home! Being the one who always has to take the initiative in my family, I suggested we go out to dinner to celebrate my success. Hey, no one else was going to suggest it – that became clear and I wasn't in any mood to cook dinner. No, I was a success, a newly Licensed School Psychologist and accomplished woman and, as such, I deserved to be waited on hand and foot. Believe it – I did. So we ventured out to The Olive Garden, one of the family's favorite restaurants, and I filled in the brood on all the details of my adventurous day in Columbus. They all listened with half an ear between inhaling those delicious breadsticks and guzzling their pops.

"Congratulations, Mom," my oldest son managed. "Now are we allowed to have dessert after dinner?"

There's nothing like kids to bring you back to reality. There's no place like home!

Chapter 13

The Beat Goes On

After passing the Licensing Exam, I returned to work in my school three days a week. It was February and I still had half of the school year to complete. As much as I was looking forward to completing the school year and starting in my Private Practice, I was also a bit apprehensive. I had mixed feelings about leaving a school I loved and where I knew people valued me. The people I worked with closely knew I would be leaving at the end of the year and many times asked me, "Are you sure?" The fact is, I wasn't sure at all. This seemed like a huge leap, especially after all of the changes our family had endured the past few years. Still, deep down in my gut, I knew it was the right thing to do and the thing I was destined to do. I never questioned the ultimate goal, but the path to get there was clearly more difficult than I had ever imagined. The journey was exhausting and many times I was tempted to throw in the towel. I was making fairly decent money, got along well with most of the faculty and was valued by parents and children. What more could I ask for? Yes, it was comfortable and fit me like a worn pair of jeans.

I had been told by many people "you are the best school psychologist this school has ever had." That is a wonderful compliment and something I struggled with. I knew the school would probably get a new person who would fumble around getting to know parents, students and faculty. In all probability they would get someone whose qualifications were questionable. That had become the norm from my employer. My sister, for one, kept telling me, "that is not your problem." Deep down, I knew she was right, but I was having a difficult time embracing that idea because I truly cared about this school. Yes, those of us who care too much are often our own worst enemy. If I didn't care so much about students and families in general, I wouldn't be determined to leave and do more. Still caring so much is what would ultimately make it difficult to leave here. My strong conviction to advocate for families in the right way was pulling me away. It was a dilemma for sure. I was finding out that dreams are scattered with dilemmas. While the ultimate dream may be crystal clear, the path to achieve it is often fuzzy, cloudy and not clearly marked. This is where faith comes in, and my faith was growing stronger by the day.

So, ultimately, I went about my job the rest of that school year, doing what I had always done – my best. At least I thought I was giving it a sincere effort at the time. Looking back I realize that maybe I was only operating at 75%. I was often distracted, wondering about the future. Still, knowing that some other people always operate on this level, I felt like I did an adequate job. Everything was accomplished, teachers and parents were pleased and service to students did not suffer. I had seen several students in counseling for years and I knew leaving them would be my biggest challenge. Establishing rapport with grade school age children is a slow but necessary process. I was working with several families that had serious difficulties in their home lives that carried over into school. Each family had two students that I worked with. Although I was making progress with all of them, one adolescent boy in particular had really come to trust me and rely on me for advice. In May, when I finally told him I would be leaving at the end of the school year, he looked up and innocently inquired, "How will I make it through fifth grade without you?" That is the ultimate compliment for any counselor since you are never quite sure you are making a difference or just wasting time. After taking a moment to digest that unexpected statement, I patiently explained that I was not abandoning him. I would give his mother, who was his only parent, my Private Practice information and she could continue to bring him to see me if she chose. I didn't offer this to many people but he and I had seen each other for two years in counseling and did have a special bond. I knew this student really needed someone he could trust since he had recently lost his father. I explained to him that it would, of course, be up to his mother but that if they wanted to continue to see me, I would make it work. When I met with the mother later and explained the situation to her, she of course was worried about whether my services would be covered by her insurance. I told her I didn't think they would be, but that she should not worry about that if she wanted me to continue to see her son. Somehow, I would work it out. I also explained that there would be a new school psychologist who could, of course, see her son, but it would inevitably be difficult for both of them since we had a long standing relationship. She said she understood that and valued my relationship with him greatly. I left that school year feeling confident she would call me and I would continue that relationship. Something similar happened with the other family, although my relationship with them was not as longstanding. Unfortunately, I never heard from either of them again. That was difficult for a while, because part of me felt like I had let them down when they needed me. Seeing me outside of school was either an inconvenience, or maybe just out of their comfort zone. Whatever the reasons, I decided in the end, it probably wasn't all about me. That is a life lesson I am learning to embrace every day. It's mind-boggling but I've come to realize that sometimes people actually make decisions without me in mind! Startling – but true, nevertheless.

Starting Private Practice was more difficult than I ever envisioned. Actually getting the office set up was the easy part. I had a friend who offered me space in a building she was renting for educational purposes and it seemed perfect. I had to invest in a conference table and a few office supplies but that was minimal. The large investment came from the test materials I would need. Working in a school setting, all of the test materials a school psychologist uses are supplied through the public school district, so this was all new to me. Of course I had thought about these costs beforehand, but they quickly added up to more than I had planned on. I tried to secure a small business grant but after many hours of researching that idea and coming up empty handed, I decided I would have to charge most of my test materials. That is not the ideal way to start a Private Practice of course but I felt sure I would re-coup my losses down the road. Yes, I was a Licensed School Psychologist, I was a family advocate and I knew about rights in education. Surely people would come flocking to me with their children, eager for my opinion on educational matters.

Within the first few weeks of setting up practice, I had my first client. This was not someone I solicited myself, but actually someone the principal at my former school sent my way. I was grateful for the referral but it was a bit sticky and I had to make sure he was an acceptable client before I begun. I didn't want any flack from my former employer at this point and thus had to explain to the girl's mother that he could be evaluated at that school in the fall if they wanted to wait. She was a girl who was going to be a new student and the principal basically wanted more information on her so that the school could best meet her needs. I had never had dealings with this family before, so there was no conflict of interest. I also covered all my bases, making sure the family knew that they would be paying for my services. I also informed them that they might want to inquire through the public school system and see if they would evaluate their daughter over the summer free. Most public school districts do not evaluate students over the summer, especially parochial students, but I wanted to operate my Private Practice on good, solid ethics. If they could get her evaluated for free, I could not justify them paying me. In the end, the public school system would not evaluate the girl and they chose to come to me to expedite things and have the assessment completed before the beginning of the school year. The mother did thank me several times for giving them all the information about what might be available to them. I basically shared what I knew and what I believed was my ethical and moral obligation to share. Some people probably would have handled it differently, but I was determined to operate my practice in an honest, forthright fashion. I firmly believe honesty is the best policy.

After that initial evaluation, things slowed down considerably. I went about doing what I had set out to do, which was basically getting the word out that I was available to do evaluations, consult with parents and go to schools on their behalf if they wanted me to. I distributed a brochure to many friends and left them in several locations around town. And then I waited and waited and waited. Nothing seemed to be happening. I was accustomed to working three days a week and being busy. This was anything but busy and, once my kids went back to school that fall, I was left with a great deal of free time. Free time I tried to fill up with household duties, reading and other hobbies while I patiently waited for clients to call me and enlist my services. I did get some calls here and there but mostly they ended up being dead ends.

A big obstacle I faced that I hadn't counted on beforehand was how to transition from an inquiry on the phone to an office visit and some revenue. Many times mothers would call me asking for advice about their child and some school issue. It sounded promising and I determined within five minutes that they and their child would definitely benefit from my services. The problem was figuring out how to get off the phone and offer the advice in my office for a fee rather than on the phone for free. When you are in a helping profession and enjoy helping people, this is a dilemma. I wanted to help and offer solutions and expertise, but I also needed money to pay rent and eventually have some left over. This was ultimately a business, after all. After one or two conversations like this with concerned mothers I decided that in the future I would have to leave the person hanging somehow, someway so that they would have to schedule an appointment at my office for more. The problem was the next time someone phoned, I found this difficult, if not impossible, to do. Several times I did manage to end in a way that I thought would secure a future relationship. "I'll really need to see some school records on your son before I can offer anything more." This typically ended with the mother assuring me that they would make an appointment and come in and see me. "Oh, sure, we will call you next week." I then went on to give them directions to the office and assure them of the days I was available. Maybe I'm gullible, but I really believed most of these people would call me. When they didn't I began to realize that I was probably giving too much information on the phone. I guess there is a fine line between giving enough information so that people know you are competent and giving so much information that there is no need to see you in person. This is one part of the whole Private Practice dilemma I hadn't counted on.

So, Private Practice was slow and I began to doubt that I would ever make a living at it. Most months I couldn't even pay the rent unless I borrowed from our personal money, which I found myself doing more and more. Still, I always believed in my dream of providing good, quality school psychology services to children and families. I knew I was good with children and I knew I had expertise to offer. I also knew that this just wasn't working the way I had envisioned. Dreams only get you so far. Mostly, I felt useless and that is never a good feeling. I knew after about six months that I needed to find some way of feeling useful again. Friends I knew who were in Private Practice in School Psychology assured me that it often takes "two-three years to build up a practice." Many had worked part-time in schools as they built up their practices. Unfortunately staying in my school was not an option as I had really wanted to get away from my employer. I had thought about seeking other employment but really hadn't tried too hard as I was convinced that the Private Practice would take off. This is where high expectation and optimism sometimes sets you up for a fall.

After sticking it out for a good nine months in Private Practice I decided to actively seek employment in a school setting for the following school year. Funds were quickly being depleted, business was not picking up and I had a daughter starting college soon. Mostly I just missed being useful to children and families. Things were not panning out the way I had envisioned, so I turned to God to help as I have many times in my life. I basically asked him to show me the way and give me a sign. I firmly believed I was meant to advocate for students and families but this avenue was not working. Should I stick it out or move on? What would He have me do? I basically asked him to lead me where I should go.

In the spring of that year I continually searched the Department of Education website for openings in school psychology. I filled out several applications and soon had an interview for a two day a week position in a school district forty-five minutes away. It seemed just right at the time. I could work two days and have an income and still try and build the Private Practice. It could be the best of both worlds. I wasn't crazy about the drive but for two days a week, I thought I could handle it. So, on that rainy day in spring when I went to the interview I was hopeful and energetic. I was rehearsed and ready with all the answers about why I was the best choice of applicants.

After I finally did locate the Board of Education where the interview was taking place, I was forty-five minutes late. I had called and spoken to a secretary fore-warning her and asking if I should re-schedule. I took a wrong turn somewhere due to faulty directions and went miles out of my way on a highway. That coupled with a severe thunderstorm had me arriving in a state of inner panic. I think I did pretty well concealing it on the outside, but let's just say it didn't start out to be a great interview.

One of the women who was obviously supposed to be interviewing me actually had to excuse herself before we began because she "had to be somewhere." I was the last interview of the day and had obviously held her up. Lateness and anxiety mixed with a little guilt could be a deadly combination for an interview. I was proud of myself, though, because despite all this I was cool, calm and collected. Yes, I needed this job and I was determined to beat the odds.

As I drove home after the interview that day, I was fairly confident the interview had gone well despite the set backs. Still, I was quite sure I wasn't going to get the job. It just did not feel right to me. I must say I really wasn't that concerned about it either. The district was far out in the country and I just did not seem to connect with the people that well. I answered the questions correctly but I did not feel a connection. Something was missing and I have learned to trust my instincts on jobs, people and most situations I have encountered in the past few years. Sure enough, I received the typical form letter a few days later, saying that they "had decided to go with another candidate despite my excellent qualifications."

Yes, I had read letters like this before. The only difference is that normally it would have really bothered me and I would have been angered, frustrated and down right upset. This time I was totally at peace with all of it. It just didn't matter because I knew it wasn't right for me and something better was coming. I believed it. I didn't know when or where but I knew it.

The next few weeks I filled out a few more job applications and was more relaxed than I had been in a long time. I had the realization that I would be employed again in a school somewhere in the fall. I didn't know where and I didn't know how but I knew it would happen. I had faith that somehow I was destined to be back in schools advocating for families. So, Private Practice hadn't worked out the way I planned. Did that mean I was just going to quit on my dream of advocating and helping kids? No way. First, it is not in my nature to quit. Secondly, I knew God was telling me to press on and He would show me a different venue. I knew it. He had taken care of everything the past few years and He wasn't going to quit on me now. No, he had seen me through all this for a reason. The reason would be revealed to me in His time, not mine. So, I prayed and I waited. I went about my daily routines without a shred of anxiety or worry. I even started running again on a regular basis. Something I had been lazy about for a while because I was stuck in the "poor pity me" phase of disappointment over my Private Practice stand still.

In a few short weeks I received a phone call that would inevitably change the direction my life would take – again. A woman I had met years earlier in a school where I worked needed school psychologists to service some private schools she was working with in the area. She had gotten my name from a former principal who thought highly of me. She basically asked if we could meet and discuss some "opportunities" she had that "might interest me." Well, of course I was curious, but mostly I was hungry for work, purpose and to get going on whatever it was God had in mind for me. Bring it on baby. You don't have to ask me twice!

We met that spring day and discussed school psychology and education in general and my views on them. She wanted to make sure I was a woman of "integrity" and would be a "good fit" for her company. I thought that was refreshing and insightful. She wasn't about to hire any warm body to fill the spot and her needs. I respected her even more from that moment on and was anxious to hear more. In the end, she offered me the position of heading up the School Psychology division of her company. It would be a new division she was starting and had chosen me to head it up. What an honor! I was flattered, of course, but mostly I felt like everything in my life had come full circle – finally. I felt like the destiny I was waiting for was coming to fruition. I had left a company because of problems with their daily practices and ethics. She knew this and was offering me a job largely because she respected me and my experience in school psychology. I was going to be a part of a company with high moral and ethical standards and integrity. It truly felt like I had been handed a gift from above. I, in fact, know I had. I would be advocating for children and families and have more control over what type of people were put into schools as school psychologists. In my position, I would in fact be hiring some of them. The joy I felt leaving that meeting on that spring day is beyond words. I knew God had orchestrated it all in His time. He was showing me in his way why I had to go through all of that. It was all so clear that I couldn't help but shed a tear or two as I drove home. A tear of gratitude for lessons learned and dreams fulfilled. A tear for people who step out and make a difference in life. Yes this was right and I felt a true sense of inner peace for the first time in years. It had all come full circle.

"All your tomorrows are in God's Hands. He who began a great work in you will carry it on to completion." (Philippians 1-6). I wasn't quite sure where this would lead, or what my future held but I knew I would be o.k.

Conclusion

The Other Side of the Table is the culmination of years of necessary changes, soul searching and growth. I hope reading it has helped you in some way. If your children struggle in school, please find the information you need and advocate for them in their educational setting. Ask the difficult questions and don't accept what you know in your heart may be wrong for them. It may be an uphill battle but it is certainly one worth the climb. You are your child's best resource. If all else fails, find the courage to walk the walk to a new educational setting. There are many excellent schools, both public and private, with excellent resources.

My sons are both doing wonderfully because I didn't accept the easy way. To date, it is the most difficult journey I have ever taken, but I truly have no regrets. My older son no longer qualified for LD services in fifth grade. He is a freshman in high school and excels in every way. He has straight A's.

I just came from a conference with my youngest son's fourth grade teachers and all three proclaimed, "We wish we had ten more like him in class. He operates on such a high level of intelligence." For someone who had heard very few positives at any conference I attended when he was younger, that was music to my ears. Although he has a 504 Plan with accommodations for Attention Deficit Disorder, many are not even necessary at this point. When I left that conference my heart was light and I gave profound thanks that we live in such an excellent school district. I am grateful for schools that strive to meet the needs of each child, and educators who go the extra mile for students and families. I think I literally floated out of that building, finally having found a sense of peace.

No one goes through life without struggles. Behind every seemingly "professional" persona is some deeply personal story. We all learn by what we experience and the challenges put before us. We each choose to either press on or give up. Whatever life throws at you, I hope you choose to press on and have faith. If you believe, He will always carry you through. Faith, Family and Friends are at the center of this story. I believe everyone needs them in their life. Seek them out when you need them and rely on the strength of others to get you through the valleys. We are not meant to do it alone. As difficult as this experience was, I believe God knew it would strengthen me. His plan is always the best plan.

Author Biography

Mary J. Shafer is a Licensed School Psychologist who has worked in education in the Cleveland area for twenty years. She holds Masters of Education and Educational Specialist degrees from Kent State University. She is the mother of four children and is passionate about advocating for children and families. Mary enjoys running, biking and listening to music. She loves writing true, inspirational stories laced with humor for women of all ages.

9 781451 585391